A *Practical* GUIDE TO
PUBLIC
RELATIONS

AMY ROSENBERG

VERACITY
PORTLAND, ORE.

A Practical Guide to Public Relations for Businesses, Nonprofits and PR Leaders

Published by Veracity Marketing
Portland, Oregon 97206

For discounts on bulk purchases or to hire the author to speak visit: **veracityagency.com**

Copyediting by Debra Flickinger, Cailyn Tegel and Mike Rosenberg

Book cover and interior design by KUHN Design Group | kuhndesigngroup.com

ISBN: 978-1-7365140-2-3 (print)
      978-1-7365140-3-0 (ebook)

First Edition

CONTENTS

For my mother, the original entrepreneur.

INTRODUCTION

Most public relations (PR) books profile famous companies, viral campaigns or jaw-dropping crises—all with unattainable resources or unimaginable situations. The picture becomes one that is out of grasp, blocking everyday people and organizations from entry.

This I take personally because I come from a family that has operated its share of small businesses. Growing up amid the scent of flowers drying on a rack, to be arranged and sold to neighboring businesses, the kitchen table was always strewn with the accoutrements of creativity.

When applied practically, PR can help businesses like these grow and thrive. In demystifying the PR process, I've tried to make a difficult field seem a little more attainable for cash-strapped start-ups, scrappy nonprofits and small and family-owned businesses. No longer will opportunities pass us by.

However, many of us—especially entrepreneurs—are prone to overly leaning in, sometimes tipping right over into the waters of distraction. It's now more important than ever to focus. With a new social media platform popping up every day, and technology evolving faster than we can think, it's impossible to do it all and do it all well. But you don't need to.

These pages may feel dense at times because you'll need background to understand how to execute or manage the work. However, I've provided ways to streamline throughout, while only offering ideas that are within reach, because after that one-shot viral idea loses steam, what's next?

Practical PR is a mindset that staves off sinking momentum. Rather than flitting about from idea to idea, you'll own your actions by planning ahead and following a schedule that includes more than just PR to drive efficiency and results. Other marketing disciplines—such as search engine optimization (SEO), content marketing and social media—are not only worked into this entire book, they're ingrained into the fiber of my approach to PR.

REIMAGINING PUBLIC RELATIONS

Before we begin, let's address the elephant in the room—declining trust in the news media. Perhaps not surprisingly, the Edelman Trust Barometer has found it dwindling over the past decade in its yearly study of public trust in business, non-governmental organizations (NGOs), government agencies and the news media.* This may cause you to second-guess picking up a book about PR.

But PR isn't only about working with the news media, it's about influencing internal or external publics to bring desired results. Gaining media coverage, through the practice of "media relations," is just one way to do this. Other PR practices include community relations, public affairs, investor relations, internal communications, influencer relations, thought leadership and more.

---

* "2025 Edelman Trust Barometer," Edelman, accessed March 3, 2025, at https://www.edelman.com/trust/2025/trust-barometer.

Also, I have only told you part of the story. Over the past decade, the Edelman studies have found the public trusts businesses more than NGOs, government agencies and the news media. This points to an emerging opportunity that may be more applicable now than ever before.

BUSINESSES RISE IN THE PUBLIC ARENA

There couldn't be a better time for businesses to command respect and attention through thought leadership—which is the practice of sharing expertise to establish credibility. Before you start feeling intimidated, thinking that thought leadership means you must command a huge team or embark on a TEDx speaking tour, know that a quieter form of thought leadership exists.

When your "owned" media is infused with notions of thought leadership, it can be rendered very powerful if "earned" media efforts are used to amplify it. Owned media includes an organization's website, newsletter, social media and "content" (blog posts, podcasts, videos, etc.). While earned media is just a new term for PR that more aptly communicates the hustling aspect of gaining attention from third-party channels, rather than paying for that attention through "paid" media.

Throughout these pages, you'll learn how to write, pitch and ultimately place owned content featuring a public-facing thought leadership slant across third-party channels that don't always need to be mainstream media. You may value a shoutout from a local school or charity website more than traditional news attention, or perhaps a social media share or a write-up in an industry newsletter is more your jam.

HIDDEN BENEFITS TO MEDIA COVERAGE

But, when focusing on mainstream media, don't let concerns about trust distract you from one of the main benefits of gaining media coverage: increased search engine optimization (SEO). Improved SEO helps search engines like Google and Bing rank your website higher in search results, making it easier for your audience to find you.

For organizations relying on online searches to connect with audiences, coverage from mainstream media websites that rank well in search engines can be invaluable. Not only do people make all types of decisions based on online searches—this is increasingly how they get their news.

Although access patterns differ across countries, the 2024 Digital News Report* found that more people—especially younger audiences—are turning to search engines and news aggregators (such as Apple News) to find news, rather than social media or going directly to traditional news sites or apps. However, that news still needs to be included on a third-party website for it to be discovered later through search engines and news aggregators.

But discovery alone doesn't equate to trust. Whether or not audiences believe the news they stumble upon online is a different matter altogether. My hunch? People are more likely to find news credible when it incorporates insights from a trustworthy thought leader—someone who brings expertise, perspective and authority to the conversation.

That thought leader could be you.

SETTING FORTH TOGETHER

Be it a means to an end, such as earning online news placements to increase SEO, or attempting to make a larger impact through thought leadership, learning how to work with the media is still a reasonable pursuit. Not to mention that gaining attention from others—call it PR, earned media, marketing or just plain hustling—has been the hardest for "outsiders" to learn and understand.

---

* "Digital News Report 2024," Reuters Institute, accessed March 3, 2025, at https://reutersinstitute. politics.ox.ac.uk/digital-news-report/2024.

In writing about the PR process, I've become humbled by the monumental amount of organizational discipline, strategic foresight and sheer time the work requires. However, the stick-to-it-ness found within the daily and overarching act of PR is the same type of stick-to-it-ness required to launch a company, stand by a mission or lead a team.

We have more in common than you might think. The PR person who is here to deepen and expand their craft can learn alongside the small business or nonprofit operator who deserves to pair their PR starting point with context, strategy and a wide range of options.

We're all in good company here. Let's embark on this journey together.

CHAPTER ONE

THINKING
BEFORE DOING

O ver the years helping countless organizations with their marketing and PR, I have not only witnessed common mistakes, I have
facilitated them. My first mistake involves getting down to work without thinking about why or who I'm attempting to reach. I'll admit, this
is exactly what I told readers to do in my first book, *A Modern Guide
to Public Relations*.

However, that book was meant to get newbies out of thinking and into
doing. Even the most experienced of us are prone to getting started so
perfectly that we never actually start. While I don't want to lead you
down the path of inaction, this more advanced book affords us room
to get our heads on straight first.

The best way to ensure you don't act too quickly, nor fall into the rut of
narrow-minded thinking, is by pausing first to consider:

- **Goals:** After uncovering your organization's goals, you can
  narrow your focus to consider how the goals of specific

departments affect those overall goals — perhaps starting with sales and fundraising, then funneling down into marketing and its ancillary functions (such as PR, social media and content).

- **Audiences:** Not only do you need to know the distinct types of audiences you'll focus your efforts on, you'll need to learn about each audience. By doing this, you may also discover ways to maximize efforts (by reaching multiple audiences at once) or narrow your focus (by prioritizing one audience type over another).

- **Campaigns:** Understanding goals and audiences can provide the starting point for a plan, which will essentially line up what to do — otherwise known as your campaigns.

START BROADLY THEN NARROW DOWN

The other common mistake I used to make was considering goals too narrowly if I even considered them at all. I would self-importantly stride into client planning meetings only to inquire about their PR and marketing goals, completely forgetting the more important topic surrounding the goals of the organization.

It may seem that the top priority for most organizations would center around increasing profits and funding. But there is always something deeper, something behind the money. An experienced team secures your funding. Quality innovation increases product purchases. Dedicated customer service commits loyal customers. Examples like these are what drive the bottom line, which means they are the more important goals.

Only when discovering what is behind the money can you leverage PR and marketing to enhance what is truly bringing your organization success. Let's examine how we can further two broad goals — workplace culture and helping others — through PR and marketing:

Workplace Culture

Highlighting positive workplace culture will boost morale and assist recruitment efforts. You can apply for awards like "Best Places to Work" to build workplace pride and attract new talent. Or you can highlight top team members to reward those who are excelling. In the coming chapters, you'll learn how to place media articles under team members' names, book them for speaking engagements, promote their achievements in the media and more.

Helping Others

Many organizations consider helping others as their ultimate aim. The product or service that a business provides will most likely fill some sort of need for other people. The same goes for the altruistic tendencies of a nonprofit's mission or cause. PR can be the secret weapon to driving demand through increased public knowledge, elevating need and more.

You may be intimidated by lofty goals that are undoubtedly hard to track. But remember they can be portioned into smaller, measurable goals. For example, the trackable goal for a social media campaign could be driving clicks to a job posting. The more clicks received, the more successful the campaign was on the surface. Of course, whether the clicks turned into valuable new hires — whose jobs further the organization's mission — is part of the larger, possibly untrackable, picture.

CHECK YOURSELF AND YOUR AUDIENCES

When outlining goals, ensure they work to serve your mission. A great way to do this is through talking with others to confirm, focus or redirect assumptions you may already hold. Even if you're the leader who sets the goals, make a habit of pulling others in to check your assumptions and get a different point-of-view.

I find that actual conversations, not email interviews, work best for gathering insight. Emails are a cold way of communicating and can feel like one more thing to do. In-person conversations allow for the magic of follow-up questions, which can bring clarity and yield new paths you hadn't considered venturing down before.

Seek out conversations with key stakeholder groups, like employees, board members, potential/current investors, clients/customers, top leaders, etc. Make sure to keep the conversation broad at first to ensure you're aligned with goals and mission. Then steer the conversation into audiences so your stakeholders can help you understand which audiences you'll target.

Understanding Your Audiences

One way to stay close to your goals is to be mindful about audiences before shaping your campaigns. If the stakeholders you're already speaking with fit any of your audience profiles, try to glean the following from them:

- What do they care about?
- What makes them take action?
- What mediums hold their attention (i.e.: social media, the news, search engines, etc.)?

Look beyond your stakeholders for insight about groups you're trying to reach. Speak with older family members to better understand the Baby Boomer generation. Or engage with younger neighbors to learn about Gen Alpha. Tap your professional connections, such as vendors, past co-workers, etc. The more you get out and about—whether virtually or in person—the more connections you'll be able to learn from.

Conduct Short Surveys

There may be times when you'll need to talk with more than a handful of people to understand more about your audiences. Survey tools bring efficiency to this process. Many groups use SurveyMonkey, which offers free unlimited surveys. No longer than 10 questions, "response limits apply," and additional perks, like analytics, are available for a nominal subscription fee.

You could "buy responses" (currently around $1 - $1.50 per response) from SurveyMonkey, which has access to all kinds of people in participating countries, allowing you to narrow down by demographic. Or get people to respond for free by sending surveys directly to contacts, posting your survey on social media, polling employees and more.

Lend a Social Listening Ear

More than just paying attention to your audiences on social media, social listening tools can help you glean trends, insights, sentiment and information about what your audience expects from your brand, while also helping you monitor your reputation.

Social media management tools, like Hootsuite or Sprout Social, include social listening basics in their packages. Or play around with a tool that has a free social listening option, like BrandMentions, as you're building your plan and understanding your audiences.

Hire a Research Partner

You may feel the need to bring in a partner to help you understand your audiences. Approach this with a modicum of control, lest you get stuck in the never-starting-realm. In reality, the best marketers are changing course as they go, leaning into what's working and dropping the rest. It can be hard to stray from research that you're overly tied to, especially if it was expensive or time consuming.

That said, there are several qualified research firms that can help you:

- Conduct focus groups to test reactions to various ideas.

- Undertake manual research through phone calls and conversations.

- Deploy surveys customized by audience type and topic.

- And more!

Hiring a research partner may have its purpose, but keep in mind that by the time you scrounge up the funding and find the right partner, you might have been able to accomplish some research on your own.

PRIORITIZING AUDIENCES

As you continue thinking about your audiences, the ideas will probably start to come. These ideas are what we'll convert into campaigns in the last chapter. Every campaign you add undoubtedly creates more work for your team and/or requires additional funds. So, getting really clear on which audiences you'll target will help keep things manageable.

I approach audience selection by first listing every type of audience I *think* I'd like to reach over the long run. I then assign a prioritizing scale to each audience. Meaning, audience A will receive 50% of the budget and/or time, audience B will receive 25% of the budget and/or time and audience C will receive the remaining 25%.

Of course, nothing is ever this easy. But I like to prioritize in this simplistic way, or at least list my audiences in order of importance, because without this direction I'm prone to hyper-focusing on just a few audiences and forgetting other important audiences. Or what is more likely to happen is that I'll get in over my head attempting to reach too many audiences, which is not efficient.

> The audience selection exercise in the last chapter has questions meant to help you outline and prioritize your audiences. In this exercise, we'll attempt to have no more than four audiences to keep things simple.

Weeding Out Audiences

When deciding between campaigns to reach different audiences, it's important to see what resources are available. One way to narrow your focus is to find out how many media outlets are targeted toward your audience. We'll learn how to build media lists soon, but it's good to know that if there aren't many media outlets relating to a particular audience, you can consider dropping this campaign, or the audience altogether.

A tool like SparkToro will help you examine the media and beyond. SparkToro "crawls countless social profiles and web pages to find what (and who) your audience reads, listens to, watches, follows, shares and talks about online." Five free searches each month will turn up an overview of this information, but you'll have to pay a modest subscription fee to get the full lists.

You could also examine how many of your varying demographics are available to reach through social advertising by reviewing audience profiles in Meta (owner of Facebook, Instagram and Threads). Meta allows for targeting advertisements toward specific demographics, like age, income, occupation, interests, neighborhood, etc. We'll cover this more deeply in Chapter 11.

BALANCING STRATEGY AND ACTION

While strategic planning is essential, it's easy to get stuck in the weeds overanalyzing every detail. The goal isn't to map out every step before acting, but to gain enough clarity to ensure your efforts are purposeful and effective. By prioritizing your goals, understanding your audiences and considering available resources, you'll create a roadmap that keeps you moving forward without unnecessary detours.

But planning is only as valuable as the action that follows. Use these ideas as a guide—applying what makes sense now and keeping others in your back pocket for later. As I lop a ton of information on you over the next many chapters, you may think that I've forgotten my initial stance of keeping things manageable and realistic. Don't worry about how you will get it all done now, just know that it will be prioritized into a plan of action later.

With that foundation in place, let's continue our learning journey by revisiting the concept of thought leadership.

CHAPTER TWO

THE ACCESSIBLE THOUGHT LEADER

If your organization sells directly to consumers, you might wonder how thought leadership fits into your strategy. While the benefits of thought leadership are extensive, a universal benefit is its ability to enhance SEO. An important part of SEO includes consistency in authorship. In SEO, authorship refers to more than just the name attached to a blog post or website page, but also whose name will appear in digital media interviews, online presentation decks and more.

But before launching in, let's settle some misconceptions. Thought leadership is not reserved for the select few at the top of the organizational hierarchy. In fact, when coming from a PR mindset, our purposes often rely on a more subtle form of leadership. Here the word "leader" means having a strong base of knowledge in one of the following three categories:

- **Industries:** Your own industry, or the industries you're serving.

- **Geographics:** Where you, or the areas you serve, are located.

- **Markets:** The specific markets you, or your clients, affect.

WRITTEN FORMS OF THOUGHT LEADERSHIP

Start small with your thought leadership journey by picking a topic you want to promote and backing it up with research. Then share that research in a format you can control—through writing, instead of speaking—especially if you are worried about being put on the spot in a podcast conversation, speaking engagement or media interview.

In this chapter, you'll learn how thought leadership pieces should be written in order for them to get placed with third-parties. The next chapter will teach you how to ask for these placements through writing quality media pitches. And finally, you'll learn how to find the contacts you'll need to approach in Chapter Seven.

Let's move forward with the first piece of the puzzle: writing quality thought leadership pieces or managing someone else who is writing these pieces for you. When attempting to garner third-party placements, your thought leadership piece must contain at least one, if not all, of the following three elements:

Numbers and Data

It's essential to reinforce your message by incorporating strong data, statistics or whatever numbers-heavy information you can find into thought leadership pieces. But keep in mind that many of us, myself included, are not numbers people. So, you don't need to analyze or interpret data to use quality research that cites and links to original sources. Just incorporate it into the writing of your piece.

Trends and Predictions

Thought leadership pieces can explore trends, predictions or a mix of both. Trends often hint at future directions, making predictions a natural extension. Even if predictions miss the mark, they create opportunities to develop another piece that revisits and analyzes what changed. If you or your leader are unsure about where to start, look to trending topics in mainstream or industry media for inspiration, or share insights from other leaders, always giving proper credit.

Opinions and Beliefs

Sharing opinions is the cornerstone of becoming a thought leader. Yet this can feel vulnerable, especially if those opinions are controversial. Fortunately, opinions don't need to be provocative right away. You can start with insights that challenge industry norms or you can highlight others' opinions—whether controversial or not—while remaining neutral, aligning with or challenging the opinions you're sharing.

TYPES OF THOUGHT LEADERSHIP PIECES

After deciding what you will hone in on, whether it's one of the elements outlined above or a combination of all of them, you're ready to set pen to paper. Below is a brief introduction to the types of pieces you can write.

Thought Leadership Blog Posts

While an entire chapter is dedicated to blog post writing, here are a few musings specifically related to research-heavy blog posts involving thought leadership.

In the beginning of this type of blog post, introduce your concept in the first few paragraphs, including a sentence or two about the research. Then summarize the data or research in bullet-points towards the upper to middle part of the blog. Take care to stay organized by using subheads that clearly separate sections—placing each point of research in the section that best addresses it.

When uploading a blog post to your website, ensure it's "written by" or "posted by" the name of the person you want representing your orga-nization—no matter who actually wrote the piece. Not only is this important for branding your leader, but consistency in authorship is key for SEO, which we'll learn more about soon.

Guest Articles and Guest Blog Posts

Written by guest authors, "guest articles" can run in newspapers, mag-azines, websites or third-party blogs (as guest blog posts). Sometimes called "contributed" or "bylined" articles/blog posts, the idea is to get the thought leader's name printed in the "byline" as the author of the piece, hopefully along with the organization's name and website link.

Placement of the author's name, and maybe their organization's name, just once in an outlet may not sound like a lot of coverage. But, it's huge. Not only do guest articles provide an opportunity to be pub-lished, an outside source is positioning the author as the go-to expert on a specific topic.

Additional visibility comes if the outlet includes the author's headshot and biography (bio) with the piece. In just one to five sentences, bios offer key messaging opportunities because they can include mentions of what that organization does, along with website links.

Above all else, guest articles need to be relevant to the readers. They should not be advertisements in disguise. No credible source will con-sider placing such writing for free. In the next chapter, you'll learn about newsworthiness and timeliness, which are concepts that can help you develop article ideas that people will want to read.

Thought Leadership "Advertorials"

If you're keen on placing a guest article with a specific outlet, you may be able to pay for it. Otherwise known as "advertorials," these pieces run in conjunction with news articles in many outlets, although they're differentiated with the subtle placement of words like "advertising," "sponsored" or "paid" near the headline.

Most notably, these pieces read like news articles, with compelling headlines that have similar themes to the non-purchased headlines surrounding them. While advertorials are purchased, the PR person or department should be involved in the decision to purchase, selecting the topics and writing the article.

Even though you're footing the bill, you'll likely have to accept the outlet's edits because they don't want these articles to be blatantly self-serving. Scrappy teams may love to hear that sometimes the outlet's advertising department will write the piece for you, but in a non-advertising tone.

There's no shame in paying for a piece that helps others or addresses a timely topic. Especially since you'll have more control over where, when and how it is placed. Perhaps you could also negotiate extras from the outlet, such as posts on their social media channels.

However, be wary of purchasing online advertorials if your only aim is to increase your website's SEO. We'll cover the pluses and minuses of doing so in Chapter 12.

FROM THE PAGE TO THE MICROPHONE

For those who want to extend beyond the written word, this section introduces the concept of podcast appearances and media interviews for thought leadership and ends with insight into speaking engagements.

Podcast Interviews

Do not underestimate the rising influence of podcasts. In 2024, decision-makers turned to podcasts for industry developments and product news 93% more in comparison to 2019, according to GWI's 2024 Global Media Landscape report. Moreover, podcasts have more influence over decision makers than ads, radio, blogs and magazines.[*]

---

* "The Global Media Landscape," GWI, accessed March 4, 2025 at https://www.gwi.com/reports/global-media-landscape?_gl=1*16r5mjz*_up*MQ..&gclid=Cj0KCQjw0_WyBhDMARIsAL1Vz-8sOxeEYhxY1Q3wdLJv0fBO9ESUd2jMOC-5YfR0RTzG8cf4-TsBqSbgaAp9vEALw_wcB.

When setting out to pursue podcast interviews, don't get overwhelmed by the sheer number of podcasts and simply give up. Chapter Seven also details how to find the right podcasts and narrow your focus.

Media Interviews

Every situation is different, but when trying to place thought leadership in the media, securing an interview isn't the main goal. Ideally, we'd obtain guest article placements (since we have more control and positioning capability with those), links back to our blog posts (for SEO purposes) and podcast interviews (for public speaking practice and more SEO reasons). Sometimes a media interview can result from these efforts.

We wouldn't turn this next best thing down unless there's the chance that something negative could arise from a media interview. Even in that case, we'd probably advise you to go in with your eyes wide open. Regardless, some great things can happen from these interviews, such as building media relationships, showcasing expertise, SEO (if that story is online) and more.

A media interview generated from a thought leadership pitch will generally focus on what was initially pitched. The media contact may want you to expand upon the entire topic or dig deeper into an ancillary point that was referenced to put color on your original idea. A conversation enables them to quote part of what you've said within a story they're working on or to get more information for further research.

Speaking Engagements

Meanwhile, for those interested in public speaking, the first step is to find the opportunities. We'll learn how to create speaking engagement pitches later. Most opportunities will come through your trade or vertical associations. Your trade is the industry you're currently working in and your verticals are the industries you want to conduct business with.

Many trade associations host a large conference or two each year, in addition to smaller events more frequently. If national, broad-reaching groups sound intimidating, they may have smaller chapters. For example, the Oregon chapter of the Public Relations Society of America (PRSA) is a more approachable option for me since I live in Oregon. You could additionally seek out opportunities through local chambers of commerce, rotary clubs or charitable groups.

You'll also want to run a general online search for opportunities. The big events should come up in a search and aren't always connected with a professional trade organization. In fact, many events are organized by media conglomerates that publish relevant industry publications or online news. So, it's worth looking into the organizing group because you could also discover media opportunities or information for your media list.

Researching Speaking Engagements

When researching opportunities, first build a list of applicable trade/vertical associations and business/nonprofit groups that host events. Then fill in with any event information you can find, such as event titles, dates, topics, locations and the contacts you'll attempt to schedule with. If there's a deadline to submit speaker submissions, it's important to add this to your calendar along with the link to upload your speaking submission.

If there isn't a speaking submission link, find a contact to pitch by visiting the contact/about us page on the event's website. If you don't stumble across the person in charge of speakers/events, connect with someone in marketing as there may be some overlap.

While a speaking engagement could fall into place during your initial outreach, you may need to work on building a relationship with the group before the engagement can be booked. The relationship could bring additional benefits, such as new business leads, contributed blog post opportunities, social media highlights, newsletter inclusions and more.

Try to build a mutually beneficial relationship with the marketing and/or events lead that is not based on asking for opportunities. Start by simply attending the group's events, being sure to arrive early and stay late to network. Meanwhile, consider volunteering, sponsoring, serving on the board or connecting the group with potential speakers, board members or volunteers who may not even be with your organization.

THE THOUGHT LEADER VERSUS THE PROMOTER

In this chapter I have addressed "you" — the reader — as if you are either the thought leader who will be promoted or the person working behind the scenes to promote someone else as thought leader.

In a small organization, it could be both. Meaning, you may be the marketing lead, working under a CEO, but you can publicly address things like culture or community, while your CEO publicly addresses topics like vision and innovation. On top of that, you may leverage other thought leaders within your organization to speak about their areas of expertise.

If you, as the top person in your organization, do not have marketing help, you can position yourself as a thought leader if you remain diligent with your plan and practice sound follow up principles. If it feels overwhelming, take a breath, and just follow the steps I outline throughout this book to achieve your goals.

Becoming a Behind-the-Scenes Champion

If you are the person behind the scenes, emulate the pep talk I've provided in the beginning of this chapter to give a modest leader the boost they need. While you'll be doing the heavy lifting when positioning someone else, you'll still rely on that leader to ensure they're able to do what you're envisioning.

The thought leader you're promoting may come in all shapes and sizes. They may not even be the CEO of your company or the Executive Director of your nonprofit. In fact, you may highlight multiple thought leaders from all parts of your organization — from the head of finance discussing economic trends and the head of human resources touching on workplace culture, to the head of science talking about innovation and the head of product development explaining upcoming trends.

It will be up to you to work with each individual to coach the best out of them for the opportunity at hand. But don't forget that your other colleagues, who are also behind-the-scenes, can lend valuable insights or information that will strengthen these campaigns.

No Heavy Lifting for Thought Leaders

Since there's nuance to positioning a thought leader, it's generally best if somebody other than the actual thought leader handles the behind-the-scenes work, such as:

- Picking topics and scheduling them for distribution in your marketing calendar.

- Writing the materials that correspond with those topics, if you cannot outsource this.

- Getting materials approved by thought leaders/stakeholders.

- Understanding where and when to promote those topics, which could include actively pitching either the media for placement or scheduling speaking engagements.

- Following up diligently to gain media placements or speaking engagements, tracking your progress and building relationships along the way.

- Coordinating opportunities between thought leaders and third-party contacts, preparing either side, as necessary.

- Following up on any post-placement needs requested by the third-party.

- Thoughtfully maintaining the relationship with third-parties to leverage additional opportunities or represent the organization well by remaining responsive and helpful.

BRINGING THOUGHT LEADERSHIP TO LIFE

Thought leadership is not reserved for the select few at the top of the organizational hierarchy. It is a strategic tool that can amplify expertise, elevate your organization's presence and foster trust among your audience.

Whether you're writing, speaking or collaborating with others, the core of thought leadership lies in sharing knowledge, offering fresh perspectives and engaging meaningfully with your target audiences. By focusing on authentic insights and leveraging the right platforms, you can create a lasting impact that extends beyond the immediate goals of your campaigns.

Next, we'll learn how to convert all these ideas into streamlined pitches to land placements. Then, we'll hone in on particular ways of writing pieces like blog posts and press releases. After that, we'll dig into the weeds of media lists before setting out to learn about each particular medium — whether that's online, print, podcasts or broadcasts. And finally, we'll touch on more technical aspects, such as SEO, AI and social media, before wrapping it up with advice on management styles and marketing plans that will keep you, and your team, on track.

CHAPTER THREE

THE INEVITABLE MEDIA PITCH

If the biggest misconception about PR is that it depends on media coverage, the biggest misconception about getting media coverage is that it depends on the press release. There's more to getting media coverage than writing press releases. Don't worry, you'll learn how to write them, but more importantly, you'll learn when your situation calls for a press release and when it doesn't.

Too often, a "yes" mentality quickly sets in when anyone requests a "press release." After the release (shorthand for press release) has been distributed, all anyone wants to know is: *did the release go out?* They often fail to ask the more important question: *What did the media do with the release?*

If the release was ignored, all that work was a waste of time, not to mention a waste of a good idea—that is, of course, if you were working with a good idea to begin with. Let's broaden our view to understand what types of stories even make it into the news, then we'll narrow down to learn which media outreach methods better serve particular scenarios.

NEWSWORTHINESS AND TIMELINESS

Most news stories contain elements of newsworthiness and timeliness. Newsworthiness connects to current events, whether in the world or a particular industry or community. This can mean tying your news to broader trends or creating your own news to garner attention. But current news changes swiftly, making it difficult to plan ahead, and poorly executed attempts to connect with certain topics can come across as crass.

Whereas timeliness considers the role of timing. From a PR perspective, timeliness could dictate the timing of your media outreach to align with editorial calendars or daily media schedules (you'll learn about both soon). It could also mean incorporating timely angles into the content being pitched, such as holidays, seasons or industry events.

THE PITCH LEADS ALL MEDIA OUTREACH

If your idea is newsworthy or timely, the many ways it could be presented to the media include: photos and videos, phone calls, event invitations, get-togethers, desksides, editorial board meetings, media drops, press kits, press releases, social media, bylined articles or blog posts from thought leaders — and last but not least — pitches.

Even though the pitch is listed as its own outreach entity, it also connects with the other outreach methods listed above because they all must be facilitated by a pitch. A pitch is just an email that's sent to a media contact. You wouldn't send a press release or photo to a contact without an email telling them about it. That is one type of pitch.

Another type of pitch is one that stands on its own, without anything else accompanying it, such as a press release or photo. If the media chooses to engage with this type of standalone pitch, you'll need to deliver what they ask for, which could morph into new ways to present the information, such as an article, interview, phone meeting, etc.

MEDIA PITCHES IN GENERAL

Media pitches provide more creative leeway than press releases and are a better option for getting out feature or trend stories rather than just the typical news of the day. But in general, think of the media pitch like a proposal in which you're asking the media to do something, such as:

- Cover the story idea that you're sending them in hopes they'll incorporate your organization/thought leader into their coverage of your original story idea.

- Include your organization in a story they may already be working on, with you becoming the "source." You can guess what they're already working on through researching their publication and editorial calendars, or considering timely themes.

- Meet with you/your team in the myriad ways you'll learn about in Chapter Six.

- Link back to a pertinent blog post or website relating to a topic they might be covering.

- Let you/your expert write an article for exclusive publication in their outlet.

The shorter the media pitch, the better. **The most important part of the pitch is the subject line, with the first sentence in the body of the email being the second most important part of the pitch.** Assuming everyone is reading pitches on their phone, they can scan part of the first sentence without needing to open your email. Be very careful with these two portions of your email.

Moreover, your pitch should change to match the press medium, for example, incorporating notes of sounds into radio pitches and visuals into TV pitches. In the following chapters, we'll dig into the inner-workings of each medium, which will bring more clarity around customizing pitches based on their nuances. Before that, let's go through the main types of pitches.

Editorial Calendar Pitches

When in doubt about what to pitch, turn to editorial calendars, otherwise known as "ed cals."

You may have heard of ed cals in the realm of content marketing, with a calendar used to track the content an organization will release. Traditional print publishers and some online media also use ed cals to map out what they will cover and when.

Ed cals are typically put together so the advertising department will have topics to tie into when selling ads. This is why ed cals are often buried in the website's advertising section, within the publication's "media kit." If you're unable to find the ed cal, email a contact in the advertising department and ask for it.

Just because ed cals sell advertising doesn't mean you always have to spend money to leverage the ed cals. Knowledge of the upcoming editorial topics enables you to reach out to the editor/beat reporter with a very simple email pitch saying something like:

> Subject Line: [Insert publication month from ed cal] Focus on [Insert topic from ed cal]
>
> Hi [insert names],
>
> I know you're covering [insert topic] in [insert issue or timeframe], and I wanted to see how [insert organization or person] could help by [insert the action you propose].
>
> We could touch on the following:
>
> - List a few bullet points here if you have more to say.
> - They could be some angles/thoughts you have on the subject.
> - And/or you could include your own research on the subject.

Here is your ending point where you almost always offer the same things: speak to us for more insight, consider running an exclusive article we could write for your publication, or link to this blog post on our website with further details.

Thanks,
Sign off with your name
And contact information

If you already know these media connections well and participate in interviews with them frequently, your pitch doesn't need to be this detailed. Just getting on their radar is good enough.

Organizing Ed Cals

In fact, pitching ed cals might be the easy part. It takes more effort to organize them in a way that will help you systematically reach out each month.

After finding the desired ed cals, do the following:

- Cull through each ed cal in search of opportunities that could be related to your organization, cause or area of expertise.

- Create a calendar of opportunities you plan to target. For us, the calendar of opportunities lives in a Google Sheet and includes the following:

  » Name of outlet.

  » Issue release date.

  » Article topic and details.

  » Deadline, if listed. If not, take a guess.

  » Contact, this may be listed somewhere in the media kit. If not, ask the editor to point you in the right direction.

» Status section. Hold yourself accountable by listing the actions you've taken on each opportunity, from the first point of contact to finally landing the article.

• Include ed cal pitch deadlines in your work calendar.

Since ed cals provide so many opportunities, have someone on your team include a standing monthly date in their calendar reminding them to check the ed cal list they already organized and pitch what's coming up. Then all they have to do is send a clear, short pitch that includes the article topic and publication date in the email subject line.

If there's anything new from your organization about the topic, include that in the body of the message after introducing the reason you're emailing. It's OK if there isn't anything new to add because you might still be able to serve as a source. You're just kind of nudging them about this and seeing if there's anything you can do to help them out.

Seasonal Pitches

For publications or other types of outlets that do not have ed cals, think and pitch seasonally, or with holidays and/or large industry/consumer events in mind. Here are a few examples of how pitches could begin with this type of mindset:

• With spring coming up, the real estate market is picking up.

• With back-to-school around the corner, brain-fueled eating is key.

• With Memorial Day approaching, road-trippers are getting their cars maintained.

• With the Consumer Electronics Show upon us, these gadgets may be of interest.

• With a new year on the horizon, here's a look ahead to....

- With this year swiftly coming to a close, here's a look back at....

THOUGHT LEADERSHIP PITCHES

You have already learned that pitches revolving around thought leaders typically aim to promote blog posts, place guest articles or schedule media interviews. While we'll study this more deeply, our focus on scheduling media interviews for thought leaders will specifically detail podcast interviews.

Pitches for Blog Posts

Before learning how to write blog posts that will resonate with search engines and the media in the next chapter, it will help to understand what you're aiming to do with such blog posts by learning how to write their accompanying email pitches.

In your pitch, quickly introduce the topic* in no more than three sentences. The second paragraph could include a few of the most compelling numbers/research in bullet points. In the end, go in for the kill, asking for these four things:

1. Take any part of this blog post to quote the author in a relevant story you may be working on; or

2. Get a fresh take on this topic by interviewing the author for more information; or

3. Link to this blog post as a reference in a story you may be working on; or

4. Run an exclusive article on this topic by the blog post author.

Link to your blog post in the beginning of your pitch (yes, your blog

---

* Don't worry about what your topics might be yet.

post will be live when you pitch it out), in addition to pasting your blog post copy below your sign-off in case the media doesn't want to click on the link. In scrolling through the email message, hopefully they'll get to your expertly written blog post and be enticed to take action.

We'll talk about how to find media contacts later, but remember you can look beyond media websites when sending blog posts out for external visibility.

Pitches for Guest Articles

There are two ways to pitch a guest article without giving other options for coverage. But first know that an article in its original form can only run in one select outlet. If you have interest from more than one outlet, you MUST modify the original article. It is unethical to run the exact same article in multiple media outlets (unless the media outlet syndicates the article themselves). Plus, running the same piece on different websites is called "duplicate content" in SEO-speak, which is also a no-no.

1. Article Synopsis Only

The first way of pitching guest articles is to individually send a brief summary of your article theme to a handful of your top contacts, asking if they're interested in seeing the piece to consider running it. Your summary can include a link to more information, such as a blog post or news article, but it's okay if you don't have anything to link to.

Since you can only get one placement per article, this first way of pitching makes the most sense, but remember it is unlikely you will get a "yes" to running the piece until your contact sees the full narrative.

2. Unpublished, Completed Article

The second way to pitch guest articles is to write the article before you even get a "yes" from a third-party contact. However, do not upload the article to your website yet! You may think it's risky to spend time writing an article without anyone agreeing to run it first. But in my experience, this method of pitching seems to gain more placements. If not, the article you wrote can be repurposed for your website, blog or other owned content.

Guest Article Outreach System

Here's how we pitch guest articles that have already been written. First, the email pitch should begin with a short article summary, followed by the guest article pasted below. Ideally, you don't need a verbose pitch because the headline and introduction of your article are so compelling.

Then, send this pitch out to five outlets simultaneously (separately, not in group emails). Even though only one outlet can run your article, approaching them one-at-a-time would take too long.

In response, if two outlets want to run the article, quickly commit to the better one, while telling the leftover outlet that it was recently committed elsewhere. Media contacts often take days to write back, so this has never been awkward for us.

But don't stop there. Tell the leftover, second best outlet that you can create another "customized" article "just for them" by digging deeper into a specific section of the original article.

Multiple contacts immediately requesting your article is a rare, best-case scenario. It's more likely that you won't hear back from anyone in the first attempt, in which case:

- Follow up with your top-five outlets two days after sending the article, saying you are going to move on to other outlets in two business days (include the date to give them a deadline).

- When the two-day grace period has passed, move on to the next five best outlets.

- Repeat the follow-up and move-on cycle.

Podcast Pitches

A podcast pitch can either emulate one of the three core thought leadership themes discussed in Chapter Two—numbers/data, trends/predictions, or opinions—or it can generally tout your spokesperson/yourself as a good interview option because of x, y and z. Oftentimes, it's a combination of both approaches, but still keep your pitch brief and to the point.

With a combination approach, ease up on the topic being pitched. It's enough to "hook" your contact with a slight mention of what your thought leader would discuss to provide more room for why this thought leader/you should either a) speak on this topic, b) appear on this podcast, or c) both.

After introducing the thought leader's credentials in the pitch, include:

- Links to bios (with a headshot, especially if you/they represent a population that may be considered diverse in your area).

- Previously recorded interviews or speaking engagements.

- Number of social media followers (if the numbers are impressive, which could vary depending on the industry, topic or caliber of podcast).

- How the interview will be promoted, whether through an active social media following, a subscriber-based newsletter, etc.

When *not* focusing on a specific theme or topic, thought leaders can be pitched just because of the mere fact that they'd be a good guest on that particular podcast. If you'll be doing a lot of general pitching, you may consider **creating a speaker sheet** that includes:

- Short bio.

- Topics you/they can discuss.

- Potential questions you/they can answer.

- Headshot and/or images.

- Links to past appearances (with comparative stats, if positive).

- How the appearance will be promoted.

Be sure to copy and paste the speaker sheet into an email message as we'd never expect a busy person to download an attachment. And while a website landing page for this speaker sheet is helpful, you'll still want to paste the copy into the email message because many people are wary of clicking on links from unknown sources.

Speaking Engagement Pitches

While speaking engagement pitches don't go to media contacts, you'll still need to put your ideas in writing and send them to people, so why not consider these like pitches as well? In fact, they can closely emulate podcast pitches, possibly with more emphasis going toward potential topics.

Come up with speaking topics by reviewing past event schedules and speaker lineups to spark your imagination, understand the event's vibe or uncover what the event might be lacking. Presenting a few topics—possibly with catchy presentation titles—will bring personality and staying power to your pitch.

Moreover, the podcast speaker sheet referenced in the previous section will come in handy here, whether you're linking to it or pasting it below your initial pitch. Whenever possible, it's important to reference past speaking experience. If there's no experience, work towards gaining it through speaking at smaller events or booking podcasts first.

PITCHING IS A PROCESS

Media pitching isn't about rigid templates or formulaic execution. Editorial calendars, seasonal tie-ins and thought leadership angles provide strong starting points, but the real magic lies in how you tailor your outreach to each contact, medium and moment.

Success comes from constant refinement. Some pitches will land immediately; others will need multiple iterations to find the right home. The key is persistence—staying observant, responsive and willing to adjust based on feedback. The more you pitch, the sharper your instincts become, allowing you to anticipate media needs and craft pitches that land.

With this foundation in place, let's learn more about how to write some of the pieces you'll be pitching—blog posts and press releases—to ensure your efforts create results.

CHAPTER FOUR

THE MULTIPURPOSE BLOG POST

Publishing new website content, like blog posts, is a big part of SEO. When posting on a regular schedule, blog posts can serve as the foundation for most marketing efforts. Not only does new content communicate to search engines that your website is active and valid, content can drive links and mentions back to your website when pitched to third parties—representing yet another way to increase SEO.

Other types of content—videos, podcasts, case studies, white papers, etc.—can also help your SEO. However, I lean more heavily on blog posts because they can be easily scanned by media contacts as opposed to the other options.

You already learned how to put pitches together for blog posts. Now it's time to understand how to write the blog posts themselves.

WRITING BLOGS THAT WORK FOR SEO

Creating blog posts is about more than just filling your website with words. From the structure of your content to how you incorporate keywords and links, each decision plays a role in creating blog posts that are not only engaging but also optimized for SEO. Let's break down the steps to crafting posts that work hard for your website and your readers.

Consider Keywords With Caution

Keywords are the words and phrases that match what your target audience may be searching for online. You want your site to rank high for particular keywords. There are myriad tools for finding keywords, such as Moz, Semrush, Ahrefs, ChatGPT and Google's own Keyword Planner tool.

However, as you write your blog post, refrain from making keywords your primary focus. The term "keyword stuffing" makes me visualize words upon words being stuffed into a piece of content without intent. Big Brother Google knows when websites are doing this, so try not to do this, or you'll have to deal with the consequences.

Instead, write with your audience in mind. What topics do they care about? What can you teach them? You can use your keyword list to generate ideas but don't be too obvious in your writing. First, just write the post, and your keywords will naturally work themselves in. As you edit, perhaps a few words or phrases can be changed to match your keywords.

Include Both Internal and External Links

Within your blog post, you may be able to link a few of the keywords or phrases to existing pages on your website that further explain the keyword topic. This is a great way to pass SEO authority between pages. Do this discriminately here as well so as not to look spammy to Google and website visitors.

More importantly, you should link to quality external websites when citing references within your own content. Doing this not only builds your website's authority, it provides value to other websites. Perhaps these websites will return the favor and link to your website, a process that you'll learn more about soon.

Get Organized With Headings and Subheads

As the words start to flow, ensure all topics are where they're supposed to be. Don't flit around from one topic to the next in the same paragraph or section. Stay organized with multiple headings and subheads, much like a traditional outline. Coherently organizing your thoughts makes it easier for search engines to find and index your post by topic so it shows up in the search engine results pages (SERPs).

The following format is customary for blog posts:

- H1 is the title or main heading of the post.

- H2 is the subhead. There could, and probably should, be multiple subheads representing the different points, topics or sections of the post.

- H3 is the subtopic. There could be a few subtopics listed underneath the subheads they match with if there's more to say.

You can keep going down the line, but your post should be easy to scan (for the human and Google eye), which includes looking uniform, or applying a system to the subheads, along with keeping your paragraphs concise.

The Longer, the Better

While a post should be easy to read, this does not mean it needs to be short. In fact, I continue to be amazed at how the looooong blog posts perform better in the search engines. We're talking between 1,500 to 2,500 words! And it's not just Bing and Google that love extra words. Well-performing content indicates that people are doing more than clicking on it. They are spending time on the page, perhaps actually reading it!

But not only is it hard to achieve that many words (even for AI tools!), it may not be necessary. Again, you want to provide value in a digestible way, without run-on sentences, rambling paragraphs and unnecessary words or phrases. User experience goes a long way toward building rapport with your audience and search engines alike.

However, when in doubt, stick to the longer version of the blog post. If an entire section or paragraph brings a new point without regurgitating an earlier point—keep it. Writing with brevity is generally a good practice, but not always for SEO.

And if 1,500 to 2,500 words sounds unmanageable, instead aim for around 1,000 words, and it's okay if you falter at around 800 words.

Use and Label Visuals

Whenever possible, incorporate visuals, such as photos, videos, charts, infographics, screenshots, etc., into your blog posts. At the very least, use a main image at the top of the post. This makes the page look better, tells a story when sharing on social media and increases SEO. Unsplash and others offer rights-free and/or copyright-free images, while Chapter 13 will cover how to use AI for graphics.

Also, add alternative (alt) text to all visuals. Alt text describes the visual for accessibility purposes, especially to help vision impaired people understand what the visual is trying to convey and why it's been incorporated into the piece. The search engines can also read alt text, therefore it helps them categorize your content, which again, builds website authority. Plus, those alt tags will help your images, videos and charts rank higher in the "image" search results section of Google.

Include Title Tags and Meta Descriptions

When uploading your blog post, consider title tags and meta descriptions. These pieces of HTML code bring an additional way to tell search engines about the content so it can be more easily organized/indexed to match searchers' intent.

Ideally only 50 - 60 characters, title tags explain the title of the web page, influencing how a page ranks for specific keywords. Slightly more in depth at around 158 characters, meta descriptions provide additional context, telling readers, and consequently the search engines, what they can expect to find if they click on the link.

Attribute the Thought Leader

Another thing to consider when uploading a blog post to your website is to ensure it's "written by" or "posted by" the name of the person you want representing your organization — regardless of who actually wrote the piece. Not only is this important for branding your leader, it lines up with Google's E-E-A-T concept.

Google's E-E-A-T

As one part of its complicated algorithm, Google uses actual humans to review content, giving them guidelines — otherwise known as E-E-A-T: Experience, Expertise, Authoritativeness and Trust — that mostly hone in on the validity of the content creator. Here's more about what E-E-A-T directs content reviewers to consider:

- **Experience:** The author/creator of the content should demonstrate direct experience with the topic.

- **Expertise:** The author/creator of the content must show deep knowledge of the subject matter.

- **Authoritativeness:** The author/creator and/or website should be recognized as a go-to source on the topic.

- **Trust:** Trustworthiness remains a key aspect, influencing how content and creators are evaluated.

Maximize E-E-A-T by maintaining consistent, credible expert representation online. Your spokesperson's name and title should appear exactly the same across all platforms. For example, list the spokesperson — not the writer—as the blog post author, so it aligns with media quotes (authority) and presentations (expertise). This consistency signals value to search engines, especially when paired with a detailed on-site bio (experience).

All of these factors work together to build trust—the last part of the E-E-A-T acronym. Google is getting smarter in its quest to become a quality search engine that provides results people can trust. So, just like PR, SEO isn't something you can "game." This emphasis on trust displays the deep connection between PR and SEO. Trust is not built overnight and both PR and SEO tend to be long-haul disciplines that take time.

Google's YMYL

In the name of trust, Google attempts to balance its influence by placing higher restrictions on topics that can significantly impact someone's life—particularly those related to health and finances. This is where another Google acronym comes into play: YMYL, which stands for Your Money or Your Life.

Google categorizes certain topics as high risk because inaccurate or misleading content in areas—such as health, financial stability, or public safety—could potentially cause real harm to individuals or society. As a result, Google directs content evaluators to apply stricter standards to content that falls under these categories.

If your organization deals with any of these sensitive areas, it's worth taking a closer look at how YMYL might apply to your content.

MOVING TOWARD THE CLASSICS

You may not have expected to learn so much about blog posts within a book about PR. But as you've seen by now, content can be presented in myriad ways, so long as it is valuable or newsworthy. We've gotten fancy by learning about specifically focused media pitches and technically written blog posts, but there is still room for the classic press release. Contrary to popular belief, the press release is not dead. It's only a matter of knowing when — and when not — to use the good old press release.

CHAPTER FIVE

THE REVERED PRESS RELEASE

There are other ways to reach out to media that don't involve trying to guess what they're covering, or pitching a specific theme or profiling a thought leader. Sometimes you're just trying to tell them what's new with you, your leaders or your organization. After all, the media covers the *news*, so what's *new* with you could be deemed *news*worthy — as long as you're telling them soon after it happens, or even beforehand, bringing us back to timeliness.

Instead of spinning out a bunch of flashy marketing ideas, first consider what's happening in your organization. Basic updates that media may cover — such as a new office location, product launch or notable new hire — could be timely and newsworthy.

These are the types of things that press releases are great for. Or if a photo better tells the story, it can be used in lieu of a press release, with a pitch of course. But you'll often employ a mixed approach. Sometimes sending both a press release and photo. Sometimes electing to schedule a meeting with the media contact instead.

We'll cover a slew of ways to reach out, but let's first dig into the storied press release.

WHEN TO USE PRESS RELEASES

While press releases are not always necessary, there are some instances when they're the best course of action for releasing general announcements, updates and news from your organization. Since their structure reminds us to quote key players and add additional details, press releases can transform a two-sentence news mention into a two-paragraph story.

Media advisories and fact sheets can also be included in the press release category. But let's not get too caught up in semantics at this stage. Read on as I go over the differences between each, including how they should be structured, along with templates.

Press Release Topics

First, let's cover what makes a good press release topic. Remember, what makes something "good" is the probability that it will get picked up in the media.

The standard press release topics listed below are ideal for gaining coverage in business sections, local community papers/sections or industry outlets. In general, you must attempt to do something within the community or industry where you want coverage. Then, the following press release topics can stem from there:

- Join a board/committee.

- Donate to a cause.

- Open a new location.

- Create a new service, product or company.

- Gain a significant amount of funding.

- Hire a notable new person.

- Construct a new development/building.

- Launch a new scientific study.

- Release results of a new scientific study.

- Volunteer in the community.

- Host an event, photo opportunity or press conference.

- Recap what you did (for events, fundraising and company results, such as growth).

Press Release Structure

At the end of this chapter, I've included press release and media advisory templates so you can visualize what I'm about to tell you. Ideally, press releases would not be longer than a page and they should exclude industry jargon and boastful messaging. Saying that you are the "best" or "perfect" is not only off-putting, your press release should mimic a newspaper article, rather than an advertisement.

While general press releases are typically written in standard paragraph format, you can draw inspiration from other types of press releases. For example, media advisories and calendar listings—typically used for events, press conferences or anything you're inviting people to—list details in "Who, What, When, Where, Why" format underneath a headline and possibly introductory paragraph.

Whereas fact sheets present key information at-a-glance, such as: the executive team line-up, product release schedules, historical information and more. You can get creative with fact sheets by incorporating headshots, infographics, charts or other visuals.

AP Style

The media typically write in Associated Press (AP) style. By doing the same, they can copy and paste portions of your release without having to change anything. But don't let AP style stop you from getting a press release out. It's not that big of a deal, especially since bloggers, podcasters and some traditional media are veering away from it.

However, there are a few AP style rules that remain ingrained into the old guard's heads. You'll notice funny ways of abbreviating states — like Ore. for Oregon and Calif. for California — along with particular ways to write physical addresses, titles, dates, days, dimensions, monetary units, months, numbers, time, percentages, etc.

The biggest rule is to only place one space between sentences. This is true for all writing today, not just marketing writing. If you are tempted to hold on to the old two spaces between sentences style, I don't want to know you.

When in doubt about how to write something, a quick online search with "AP style" written near your conundrum will generally pull up the answer. But it doesn't hurt to keep a copy of the latest *AP Stylebook* next to your desk. It can be purchased at: apstylebook.com.

The most important point to remember is that if AP style is stopping you from finishing your press release, just forget about AP style and get the dang thing done.

PRESS KITS AND VIRTUAL PRESS ROOMS

Many people who don't understand PR believe they must have a press kit before getting started. Let me correct them. No one needs to waste time building a press kit in the beginning. They first need to start getting media coverage, which can be generated by all the other ways I've outlined and will continue to outline. But, after building a solid PR foundation, enough may have been compiled for a press kit.

Ideas for press kit contents may include:

- Fact sheet about the organization or event(s).

- "General" press release on whatever the news of the day is. This might be your rotating press release that is constantly updated with new information depending on what you're trying to promote.

  » For events, this is the basic press release that offers the highlights in paragraph style.

- Past coverage or press releases.

- Background sheets. You could have one for each of the following:

  » History/timeline.

  » Top executives and/or board members and insights each person can offer.

  » List of products with descriptions.

  » List of services with descriptions.

  » List of partners (charities, sponsors, etc.) with descriptions.

  » Infographics.

  » Photos/videos.

- Make sure your contact information is on every single document.

If you're going to the trouble of compiling a press kit, at the very least have it uploaded to a virtual press room on your website. You can also print the contents and stuff them into an old-school folder to create a leave-behind. However, do not throw everything onto a thumb drive. Media contacts will just lose the thumb drive, never even bothering to look at it.

THE IMPORTANCE OF APPROVALS

We've been focusing on some very copy-heavy ways of obtaining media coverage. But before we move into other territory that involves visual aspects, or meeting with the media, let's touch on approvals.

If you are not the ultimate boss, you'll need to get the majority of your media materials approved before releasing them. Even bosses may need approvals when quoting someone else or including unfamiliar information. This is especially true for press releases, media advisories, fact sheets, bylined articles (approved by the "author" of the article and the ultimate boss) and blog posts.

There's a little bit more leeway with pitches, but if they contain specific details, it might be wise to have someone else check them over. Beyond obtaining approvals, having someone (who is not the original writer) review your materials is a good idea.

PR firms file away approvals from their clients for safekeeping. You may want to do the same. Especially save approvals from people outside of your organization. I have never had to access a past approval that I saved, but it's better to be on the safe side.

GENERAL PRESS RELEASE TEMPLATE

FOR IMMEDIATE RELEASE

HEADLINE: USING AN ACTION STATEMENT, CLEARLY STATE THE NEWS IN A COMPELLING OR TIMELY MANNER

Subhead (secondary header listed under the main header, not always necessary)

[City, State—Distribution Date]—Introduce your news here in the first paragraph. Possibly think of this in a *who, what, where, when, why* format—paragraph style. *What* is going on? *Who* is involved? *Where* (area or population) does this affect? *When* did or will this happen or another timely piece?

Possibly the *why* or even more specific *who, what, where, when* details would fall here, in the second paragraph. It's okay if you don't hit all of these points.

"You would include your first quote either here or in the second paragraph if it makes more sense to encapsulate your details in a quote," said first and last name, title, organization. "Do not bury your quote too far down and follow this exact format. Never bury a first quote inside the words of a bulky paragraph either, make it stand out as its own paragraph."

More specifics here, if necessary. You could further explain *why* with some supporting research, although quotes are also good places to detail *why* if you don't have research. I personally don't like a press release that simply lists quote after quote. I guess you could do this in a pinch or when working with multiple parties that must add their two cents.

"Here is where your second quote could go. You could either further explain something by quoting the same person, in which case you'd end the quote with just their last name because you don't need to re-introduce their organization and title," said last name. "Or you could introduce another person, such as a sponsor. It might be very important that the sponsor is included in the actual news that results from this press release, in which case, quote them first."

You can end here with the boilerplate or add more information here. While you can have more than two quotes in a press release, just remember that the farther down the eye travels in the press release, the less likely your external parties will get included in the actual news.

We end with the classic boilerplate. "Boilerplate" is code for copy that is the same in every document. It shouldn't be much longer than five lines explaining what your organization is about, who it serves, its products or services, website link and social media handles.

# # #

MEDIA ADVISORY/CALENDAR LISTING TEMPLATE

FOR IMMEDIATE RELEASE

HEADLINE: USING AN ACTION STATEMENT, CLEARLY STATE THE NEWS IN A COMPELLING OR TIMELY MANNER

Subhead (secondary header listed under the main header which goes into greater detail if necessary, which it isn't always)

[**City, State — Distribution Date**] — Followed by an introductory paragraph if you want. You might not even want to list the Distribution Date if you are announcing multiple dates in a calendar listing. I sometimes find that confusing. You might just want to focus on the date(s) you are announcing. So, you'd just start with the City, State and forget the Distribution Date.

WHAT: Concisely state what is happening. Try to hook media by painting a visual of what they'll see (important for TV and print photographers), capturing the sounds they'll hear (important for radio) and/or tying in what is newsworthy or timely about what you're sending them.

WHEN: Include the date and time the event is occurring.

WHERE: Think beyond only the address. Include special instructions for where media can park, clearance for live truck towers, etc.

WHY: If you are incorporating a charitable cause, include it here (as well as in the header or "What" sections, because remember people might not read this far down), along with any newsworthy or timely bits you've included up top too.

WHO: This can be a nice place to list sponsors who are paying to be in your press release. However, if they are presenting sponsors you must include them once in the event title in the first paragraph, not necessarily in the headline. You can also provide more information about who is organizing your event or more about the event's beneficiary. This section can also include any prominent people expected to attend.

Boilerplate: you don't always have to use one in media advisories. Use a boilerplate if it balances the release or adds additional background.

# # #

Insert your contact information at the end of all types of releases. Include your name, organization and the number where they can reach you — ideally a cell number.

CHAPTER SIX

ADDITIONAL OUTREACH METHODS

I n the world of PR, it's easy to lean on the written word — press releases, blog posts and carefully crafted email pitches. But there's a whole world of media engagement that goes beyond copy, and these alternative methods can capture the media's attention in powerful ways. That said, even the most innovative approaches often come back to the same basic principle: putting things in writing.

No matter how compelling your photos, videos or in-person meetings may be, people can only retain so much information. Ultimately, most media contacts will ask for key details in written form — whether to organize their thoughts, confirm facts or move a story forward. But more than that, email can be the initial gateway to another action you'll take with a media contact.

In this chapter, we'll dive into the many strategies you can use to engage the media, from leveraging visuals to arranging the right type of meeting. Each approach serves a purpose, but they all work best when combined with thoughtful, well-timed communication — often in the form of a simple, yet effective, email.

PHOTOS AND VIDEOS

Not only do most people look at photos instead of reading the actual words of an article, you can obtain twice as much media ink when incorporating photos with copy. Get used to taking photos and videos or directing others—even clients and bosses—to take them if you can't.

Not only will print and online media sources run photos, with or without your press release or pitch, TV will even run photos or video taken by non-media members, especially if they are interested in your story but don't have the staff to cover it fully. Moreover, glossy print magazines, like *GQ* or *Women's Health*, place a huge emphasis on photography, many times over content.

For the most part, your team can take photos and videos of daily happenings within your organization for both social media and news media coverage. However, some instances call for a professional photographer/videographer, including:

- **Products:** Hire a professional to shoot new products when they are released, even if only once.

- **Events:** You'll reap the rewards of having the event shot during the first year, if not every year depending on budget and event scale. Use these assets to promote the event the following year.

- **Fundraisers:** You might want a professional capturing your fundraising event, along with VIPs at the event, such as top sponsors and donors.

- **Headshots:** Get professional shots of executives you'll be highlighting in the news, especially if the headshot will be used often.

You can use a good quality smartphone to take photos of anything else yourself. See specifics on how to take and deliver photos/video to TV in Chapter Ten.

Photo Captions

Always include photo captions when sending visuals to the media. Photo captions are a great way to make more out of visuals and are sometimes the only way your organization will be included in the coverage.

The photo caption shouldn't be more than two sentences. List who's in the photo from left-to-right. Include job titles only if they are very important or you don't have much else to say. If your picture depicts a large group of more than five people, identifying each person is unnecessary. Simply summarize who they are and what they're doing. Definitely include the organizations they're with.

And finally, add a sentence that incorporates the results of what was happening in the photo if possible. X pounds of garbage collected, X dollars raised or new office opened in X community.

THE TELEPHONE

Yes, unfortunately there are still times we must call the media. First of all, anytime you want broadcast coverage you have to call to follow up on the email you initially sent or it probably won't get included even as a possibility for running. I have a system for this I'll explain in the TV and radio/podcast chapters.

Moreover, if you believe a specific print or online outlet would be interested in covering your story, you can most definitely call to follow up. In doing this, you may gain valuable information, including:

- Being pointed to a new contact.

- A slight tweak in what you presented, therefore requiring you to provide new information.

- Next steps, such as setting up an interview or sending a visual.

- A simple request to resend the information since they never received it.

- A straight-forward "no," which you can receive gracefully since it gives you closure.

  » If your contact seems chatty, listen closely as they tell you what they would be interested in covering next time.

Don't get too nervous to call print/online, because you most likely will not reach anyone, but at least you tried and can move on. However, if you really have a bee in your bonnet, you can call around the newsroom because maybe you just have the wrong contact.

Also, I know that video calls are very popular, and you might set one up later with your media contact, but right now we're talking about calling media out of the blue. Therefore, you wouldn't have the opportunity to set up a pre-arranged video call. If you've gotten that far, you're likely in the interview stage, and calling out of the blue is unnecessary.

EVENT INVITATIONS

If you are hosting an event that may interest a particular media contact, it may be worth inviting them. For instance, your organization may conduct a class aligned with your media contact's beat (coverage area). Or a new location may be marked by an unveiling or grand opening event, which could also incorporate media events, tours or photo opportunities. Or a trade organization may host a networking event full of potential media sources.

If your organization isn't directly involved in an event, you may still be able to invite media contacts who may be interested. For instance, the local rotary may host a speaker that covers your media contact's beat. Ask them to join you for the discussion to support them and build your relationship.

Get Togethers

While most media don't like large gatherings, getting together in a small group or one-on-one with a print/online contact is not uncommon. If they cover a beat directly related to your organization, ask them to join you for coffee, happy hour, lunch or a Zoom conversation (since you're not "pitching" anything, a Zoom conversation could be doable).

You may be the leader (or source/expert) of your organization, in which case it's perfect for you to initiate and attend this get-together. But if you're setting media interviews up for others, don't shy away from attending *without* your boss/leader/client. Attending by yourself can build rapport, which is important if you work closely with the contact. Or you can bring your boss/leader if you think it would be helpful. I have done it both ways, depending on the situation.

You will not necessarily pitch anything to your media contact during this casual get-together. Instead, you'll ask them what stories they're looking to cover and how you can help them, which includes understanding their deadlines and their favorite ways of communicating. If the opportunity presents itself during your get-together, you can casually mention what you have to offer as long as it's not too pushy.

Desksides

Some people try to arrange what they call "desksides"—visits to the reporter's newsroom at a prearranged time to talk about something specific. You could also consider these as brief "meet-and-greets," which may even be done virtually.

EDITORIAL BOARD MEETINGS

And finally, you can request an editorial board meeting with a local/regional newspaper to get across your point-of-view on topics like legislation, education, regulations, safety, etc. Editorial boards are made up of reporters/editors who determine their outlet's position on issues.

These positions are likely infused into the outlet's editorial coverage of the issue.

Attending an editorial board meeting can help you influence the editorial board's opinions, ideally in favor of your position, or at least move the coverage in a more favorable direction if they oppose your viewpoint.

MEDIA DROPS

Media drops are a fun way to grab the media's attention while getting a sense of where they work. Think of a unique item to "drop" by newsrooms that connects with your campaign. Include a personalized note, possibly with press materials attached.

The media drop should be exactly that—a "drop" by. You never ask to see the press contact as that would annoy them. However, if you are far away or just too busy, you can also have the item mailed to the contact.

Media drops could run the gamut from food or product samples, a gadget donning your logo or something quirky that grabs their attention with the press materials attached. But make it interesting or useful. While it may seem ideal to give press materials with gifts attached to them, remember, the media receive many trinkets.

We can look at "snail mail" in the same vein. Because the media receive a boatload of emails, an old-school letter might ensure that your press release is noticed above the 50,000 other pitches that have been emailed on that day.

PURCHASING COVERAGE

It's pretty customary to negotiate media coverage into a standard TV commercial or print advertisement buy. Some marketers even decide to do away with traditional advertising and go straight to purchasing what appears to be earned media coverage through options like advertorials in print/online media or TV segments that run in lifestyle TV news.

While you wouldn't necessarily have to pitch reporters and editors to secure purchased coverage, you might collaborate with them after it has been organized, especially in TV. I will explain more about this in Chapter Ten.

Advertising in a news-friendly way is just one option. Many marketers go beyond simply spending money, blending earned and paid media for maximum impact.

PRESS RELEASE DISTRIBUTION SERVICES

You will notice that press release distribution services are not listed as a media outreach method. Sometimes mistakenly called "the wire," you can pay services like PR Web and PR Newswire to distribute press releases to media outlets.

The downside of such services is that they typically only send your news to general newsroom email addresses, rather than directly to contacts. And not all media outlets sign-up to receive press releases from distribution services. Moreover, the results that these services promote are inflated, if not completely false. The long list of where your press release ended up running will likely be full of obscure websites that didn't hit your audience.

Sometimes services can generate coverage on more well-known websites. But when searching for this coverage through media outlet homepages, I often can't find it. Is that because the coverage reported by the service lives on a landing page that can't be accessed through the media website?

Regardless, I am not a technical person, so I just take care when deciding whether to use a service. If you're wondering if a bunch of random links on websites that are hidden is good for SEO—just, no.

However, public companies are required to make their news available to everyone, so some use these services, sometimes in addition to conducting hands-on PR. For such cases, one of the better distribution services is PR Newswire. More expensive than PR Web, the membership fee is a couple hundred dollars, and distribution fees (currently) range from the $300s to over $8,000 to deliver a press release, depending on how far-reaching you'd like to be.

BUILDING YOUR CONTACT LIST

Without a press release distribution service that will do the dirty work for you, it's time to learn how to find these elusive media contacts the right way. Detailed research will help you get to the right contacts and shape your PR campaigns as you discover more.

In fact, you may want to start by building your outreach list before getting your pitch or content together. As you research targets, you may gain new ideas or clarity—bringing a plan into focus or shifting your original ideas.

Let's get ready to roll up our sleeves and create meticulous contact lists!

CHAPTER SEVEN

BUILDING MEDIA LISTS

If you are deep into the media relations side of PR, maintaining media lists can be the most important part of your job. To say that it takes a long time to find outlets and contacts is incomplete. As media lists are constantly refined, the task is never complete. Not only do newsrooms change, but you'll find better outlets and contacts as you pitch and follow up, while customizing a variety of lists depending on the campaign.

Therefore, the media list is the hub of all PR work and it should be organized accordingly, not just with detailed media contact and outlet information, but also as a project management tool that tracks actions and outcomes. Before discussing all that, we'll dig into the most elusive part of PR first—knowing where to send your pitch.

The method for finding the right contacts involves a combination of online research and using media database software if you have access to one. Media database software provides the contact information for media outlets worldwide—allowing you to search, build customized lists and possibly even reach out to contacts through the tool. These tools can also help you find and report media coverage, depending on the level of service you choose.

While our work at the PR agency relies on the help of a media database, most instances do not call for one, especially if you work within the organization that you're conducting PR for, rather than working for several clients at an agency. But even with the help of a media database, good PR people (even at agencies) still turn to the internet to refine their initial media database findings.

START BY FINDING OUTLETS, NOT CONTACTS

Whether searching online or in a media database, I always start by building a list of outlets, rather than digging into one outlet at a time to find contacts. After creating a solid outlet list, I then investigate each outlet to find contacts who may be interested in my campaign.

While you vet each outlet to determine if it should be on your list, you may stumble upon an appropriate contact or story idea for that particular outlet. By all means, add it to your list. I just don't want you to get distracted. Finding contacts is sometimes harder, so we want to at least get one thing done—building the outlet list.

When conducting an online search, I use qualifying words to designate that I'm looking for traditional media. Below is an example of three separate Google searches I would run for the same category. Most of the results would be the same, but an outlier could materialize by searching a different way.

- Healthcare "Publications"

- Healthcare "Outlets"

- Healthcare "Magazines"

Healthcare is just an example of the industry/topic that can be inserted before the words (publications, outlets and magazines) meant to indicate that we're not searching for any old healthcare topic. We want a list of media outlets about that industry/topic instead.

I begin by searching on regular old Google. Then, I switch to the news aggregator, Google News, to see if a story pops up that's from a source I don't know about. But since Google News links to stories instead of media outlets, I'll try and get the most out of regular Google.

Weeding Through Outlets

In general, less is more when building media lists. We're not in the business of flooding inboxes with junk mail. We're in the business of pitching news the media will find useful and incorporate into their coverage.

To streamline your approach, start by removing irrelevant outlets to eliminate the need to vet irrelevant contacts later on. An online search about a questionable outlet can help you decide to keep or delete it. Most outlets will tell you what they cover on their homepage or "about" page.

Even if an outlet covers a topic you're interested in pitching, you'll want to ensure that outlet reaches the right audience. Major audience distinctions include:

Geographical Areas

If you only need to reach people in your neighborhood, you don't need to build an international list. Outlets can specifically cover just one neighborhood, while others may broaden into covering cities, states, regions, nations and even the world. This is the easiest, and most important way, to keep a clean list.

Consumer Audiences

The most basic way to distinguish between consumer-targeted outlets is by topic. For example, if you're trying to pitch a makeup product, you may keep a fashion outlet onboard, but you'd probably remove a consumer-related car outlet.

On the surface, you may not think of business people as consumer audiences. But business people consume products too. I consider general business outlets geared towards general business people to be consumer facing. *Forbes* is a national example, while the *Portland Business Journal* is a local example.

B2B Audiences

We move away from the consumer designation when considering the business-to-business (B2B) dynamic, which is when businesses are trying to reach other businesses or business people. Consumer business publications may suffice when promoting a B2B organization, but you'll also want to uncover niche outlets focused on particular industries.

B2B industry outlets can be further distilled by trades versus verticals. Trades reach the audiences you work within (PR or marketing for me) and verticals reach the audiences you service or sell to (real estate companies for me).

Covering Your Bases

Online searches may not uncover obscure B2B publications. However, if SEO is a goal, you may not need to know about outlets that don't show up in search for the topic they typically cover. But if you want to keep digging, below I've included the steps you can take to ensure everyone's invited to the party.

Revisit SparkToro by comparing what you already have on your list with what comes up in its free trial. And/or use a free trial with a more traditional media database. Note that the media database my firm uses, MuckRack, does not offer free trials.

Revisit the websites of industry associations and conferences. Not only could the industry association have its own newsletter, podcast or magazine, it may point to additional outlets. Moreover, some conferences are connected to publishing conglomerates, therefore their outlets (mostly trade magazines) will be referenced on their websites.

SEARCHING FOR TV NEWS STATIONS

When working in a new location, I love searching for TV news stations using Google. To begin my search, I already know that large to medium-sized U.S. markets should have around four TV news stations. Local U.S. TV stations are assigned to the following affiliates: ABC, NBC, CBS and FOX. If you've uncovered all four affiliates while searching, you have your TV list for that market.

If one of the affiliates is missing from this initial search, you may want to search for it separately. For example, if you notice that ABC is missing, search "ABC affiliate in [city]." The missing affiliate may not come up in a small to medium-sized market, indicating that less than four TV affiliates may exist in that area.

There may be a few stragglers that come up, for example CW. Don't ask me what CW is. I don't get news traction from this station. Sometimes CW will re-run news from the big four affiliates, so focus on the big four affiliates. Also, public broadcasting service (PBS) stations are stragglers in the sense that they're so hard to get on. While I hardly ever pitch it, the local version (Oregon Public Broadcasting in my state) is on my list.

SEARCHING FOR RADIO NEWS STATIONS

Searching for news radio is not as straightforward. All kinds of radio stations can appear in a Google search, even if you indicate that you're looking for *news* radio. During an initial search, you're likely just looking for news radio stations, unless you're handling very consumer-oriented news, such as public events.

In each city, only a couple of radio stations may be solely focused on news. There are only two radio stations that we pitch in my mid-market city of Portland, Oregon. But about 40 stations come up when I search for "Portland news radio stations."

Ultimately, searching for radio stations can be cumbersome. Unless you already know the stations in the locale where you are searching, I suggest skipping radio. In fact, we rarely pitch radio for reasons I'll get into later.

SEARCHING FOR PODCASTS

With an increasing number of podcasts covering thousands of topics, you'll have to place strict parameters around which podcasts you'll target. Even with the support of a PR software, you might first turn to good old Google and podcast listening apps, like Apple Podcasts,* to build your list.

Searching by subject, once you've identified podcasts, visit each podcast's website and/or podcasting app page to check for two things:

1. Is the podcast still releasing episodes? Make sure you don't pitch a podcast that hasn't released an episode for more than a year! If they are releasing new episodes, note how often they release, total number of episodes each year and the longevity of the podcast.

2. Does the podcast interview guests? Do not pitch a guest to a solo or roundtable podcast. If the podcast features guests, determine if you or your proposed guest fit their criteria.

After these steps, you can continue narrowing down by reviewing the following data:

- Reach (downloads and listens).

---

* The biggest listening platform is Apple Podcasts, which hosted more than 2.7 million of all the world's podcasts in March of 2025, courtesy of Daniel J. Lewis. "Apple Podcast Statistics," Podcast Industry Insights, accessed March 4, 2025 at https://podcastindustryinsights.com/apple-podcasts-statistics/.

- Number of Apple Podcasts ratings and stars.

- Number of Apple Podcasts reviews and sentiment.

- Apple Podcasts popularity (0 - 25, but only relative to other similar Apple Podcasts podcasts).

- SoundCloud or other platform followers.

- Podcast website domain authority, link opportunities, social reach, etc.

Once this data is in your spreadsheet, assign a subjective one to five priority score for potential targets and pitch accordingly.

Podcast Contacts

Unless the podcast is operated by a media outlet, contacts at podcasts aren't your usual media types. Hopefully the website of a non-media podcast will give you an inclination about who to pitch. Many podcasts are run by businesses, so even emailing an info address will likely find its way to a decision maker, whether it's the host, producer or an assistant.

FINDING MEDIA CONTACTS

With a good outlet list in hand, now is the time to search for the best contacts. Again, do not fear if you don't have a media database. You can often access a better list of contacts through each outlet's online roster, sometimes updated more frequently than media databases. Even PR people who have access to media databases should verify contacts by scoping them out online.

The newsroom roster can be found on the "about us" or "contact us" pages, if it doesn't have its own page. When reviewing the roster, ensure you're looking at the editorial side of the newsroom rather than the management side. Instead of publisher or account executive titles, you're looking for editor or reporter titles.

Your list could include multiple contacts from just one outlet. News departments work in teams, so cc'ing multiple contacts from the same outlet might be beneficial. Additionally, you may not know who you're going to pitch yet. Add good possibilities to the list now and remove them as you learn more.

Many newsroom rosters will not directly list their staff's contact information. That's okay because all you're doing at this juncture is pulling names and titles. Later you can do some additional sleuthing, such as:

- Glance at your contacts' stories to see if their contact information is included, often it will be listed at the end of the article.

- Review email address configurations listed on the website and guess what your contacts' email addresses might be.

- Call the **newsroom** and ask for this information, or simply ask to speak with your contact.

If a **newsroom** phone number is listed for TV, radio or newspaper, jot this down. In the future, you'll be calling the newsroom, rather than the general phone number. If you must call the general phone number, ask to be transferred to the newsroom. Or better yet, ask them for the newsroom number so you can call it directly in the future.

Beat Reporters

For all mediums, you'll want to add "beat" (area of focus) reporters that cover your topic. A typical beat at a general daily newspaper could be: business, politics, investigative, crime, entertainment, food, etc. The larger outlets will have more coverage areas, such as: energy, technology, education, health, music, etc.

TV and radio like to think they have beat reporters. But most reporters in these mediums are assigned to cover breaking news, rarely free to cover beats. However, larger TV stations may have a dedicated business reporter and/or someone that covers both breaking news, along with a beat like education.

CC'ing the Bosses

In addition to beat reporters, add editor titles to your media list. Including the editor on a pitch to a beat reporter is not rude or going over anyone's head. If your story pertains to what their outlet covers, the editor can redirect your email if you have the wrong contact or they're out.

Or before pitching, you could ask the editor who the best contact for your particular story might be. Hopefully, the editor will appreciate your due diligence and direct you to the right contact.

There are a variety of editor titles, including: managing editor, associate editor and more. Smaller publications may only have one editor, who may also be the reporter, therefore you'll only work with this person, whereas other publications will have an abundance of editors.

I am not too proud to 'cc multiple editors (and reporters) on a pitch. But I will be careful not to 'cc anyone too high up, going for medium-level titles and even the lower sounding titles (such as associate/assistant editor) as they might have more bandwidth to help.

Large beats may have an editor overseeing one department within a newsroom. For example, a business editor. You'd send business news to this person, rather than the overall editor.

Be mindful that many editors and reporters are also in charge of their publications' websites. This can lead to fancy and creative titles. For example, my state's daily newspaper, *The Oregonian*, attempted to include "producer" into editor titles. But they recently converted back to previous titles, perhaps realizing how confusing those terms were.

TV and Radio Contacts

When researching a new location, we don't worry about specific contacts at TV and radio stations in the early stages of list building. This is because most stories run through the newsroom, either to be axed, given to a reporter, assigned to a camera person or most likely ignored.

Therefore, the most important email address and phone number at TV and radio stations is for the newsroom. You'll know you have the newsroom email address when you see email configurations like: news@ insertstation.com or thedesk@insertstation.com. "The desk" is news jargon for the desk where decisions are made in the newsroom.

You'll learn more about how to break through to the newsroom soon.

ORGANIZING YOUR MEDIA LISTS

If you've been working with the media for a while, you may be tempted to store your contacts in your digital address book or even in your head. Don't do this! It is essential to maintain this information in a program that can be easily accessed and shared when necessary. Even if you work independently, there may come a time when you need to share your contact list with a client or a colleague.

Moreover, maintaining a list keeps you organized and ensures you don't overlook a contact. Lists can help you seamlessly transition between different audiences, topics or mediums (such as TV, radio, print, etc.)—especially when segmenting each category into separate lists or spreadsheet tabs.

Our media lists include designated "status" sections to record actions taken with media contacts—from the initial outreach and follow up stages, to scheduled interviews or bylines, to final story placement. This includes jotting down the dates of each action and what happened, for example did we leave a voicemail, speak with the contact or simply resend the email?

RESEARCHING CONTACTS AND OUTLETS

After pulling names and contact information, you might even dig further to uncover what your targets are covering. Getting a feel for each contact's tone and interests enables you to tailor your pitches or refocus your ideas. Be sure to make corresponding notes in your database/spreadsheet list.

Working in Google News

Google News provides a great way to see what your contacts and outlets are covering. It aggregates stories from news sources, organizing them in a way that is more visually appealing and easier to digest. Also, Google News apparently links to vetted news sources, whereas regular Google might link to a website operated out of your next-door neighbor's basement.

It's really important to stay up-to-date with news trends, especially within your unique niche or location. By signing into your Google account, you'll be able to customize your own version of Google News the following ways:

Local News: Depending on what you want to track, you can save just one or multiple locations in this section. This is very helpful if you're attempting to garner local news in multiple cities.

For You: This section compiles information that Google thinks you'll be interested in based on your previous search patterns, which is helpful if you search Google about topics you want to promote.

Following: Here you can follow topics, sources and locations. Don't get too excited if you want to follow an obscure topic. It seems that you can only follow more general topics right now. But following sources might be a great way to stalk before you go in for the kill.

Chapter 11 will touch on ways to use social media for researching contacts, outlets and/or story ideas.

USING MEDIA DATABASE SOFTWARE TO BUILD LISTS

And finally, here are some thoughts for those of you who have media database software. While they aren't necessary, media databases provide information about high profile outlets that do not list their newsroom rosters online. Even if the contacts found in a media database aren't completely accurate, you're at least provided some names and phone numbers that can be refined as your research progresses.

Don't build lists the way the media database trainers tell you to, which is to search for contacts first. For example, if you're working in Atlanta for the first time, they'll tell you that searching for all the editors in Atlanta will turn up everything you'll need. The idea is that since each editor's profile includes their publication, all of the outlets available in Atlanta will automatically turn up.

But what if an important outlet doesn't appear in a search because they don't have the exact title or beat topic you've input? Instead, I like searching for outlets first because each will have their own way of titling employees. While it may take a little bit longer, it seems more prudent to know which outlets to target. Then, cull through the contacts at each outlet to determine who to add to your contact list.

BRINGING LIFE TO MEDIA LISTS

Now it's time to bring life to media lists by learning about the very media outlets and contacts you'll be researching. First, we'll start with print and online media, then we'll move into radio and podcasts, and finally end with the beast that is television.

CHAPTER EIGHT

UNDERSTANDING PRINT AND ONLINE MEDIA

I have already outlined a few ways to obtain print and online media coverage in this book—from bylined article and blog post placements to writing pitches and press releases. However, we have yet to cover the distinctions among certain types of print outlets. Plus, you'd be working quite blindly without a handle on the varying deadlines you must follow to make it into a publication in time.

So, let's take a journey into the weeds of print and online media now.

THE DIFFERENCES BETWEEN PRINT AND ONLINE MEDIA

On a basic level, there are no differences between online and print media when you consider that most print media also have websites. If online visibility is part of your strategy, you might want to remove print outlets that don't have websites from your media list.

For smaller community papers and vertical/trade publications that have websites, your story may need to run in print before it will be uploaded online. In this case, follow all the same guidelines about how to get placements within the print versions of these websites.

But at some large consumer magazines and bigger daily newspapers, not every story that makes it online will also be included in print. You could try and find out, or just operate as you naturally would when trying to get a print placement and see if it also ends up online. Learn and record the nuances of each outlet as you discover their unique patterns.

If you're really after that online coverage, you could pitch the story directly to digital editors/reporters at a publication, or at least 'cc them when pitching their print counterparts.* Or if your story runs in print, but not online, nudge the digital editor to see if they'd be willing to include it.

Digital-Only and Digital-First Media

Meanwhile, some "print" outlets have completely forgone printing, opting to go digital only. While their deadlines might be quicker than traditional print deadlines, there isn't much of a difference in how you'd work with contacts at online-only outlets compared to print.

The same goes for hybrid or digital-first models. For instance, a "daily" newspaper may still consider itself a "daily," but they only print select stories a few times each week, thus calling themselves "digital-first." What's leftover is reserved for their website, with stories being uploaded sometimes on an hourly basis.

Follow the same rules and ideas for working with digital-only or hybrid models as you would for daily print models.

---

* Again, only 'cc groups of people that work in the same organization. If you must send a mass email, send it to yourself and then bcc everyone.

TV and Radio Station Websites

While the methods of securing print versus online coverage can be somewhat interchangeable, this is not the case with TV and radio because they operate much differently.

For example, when pitching print media, you may not have to follow a different method for getting on their website, other than reaching out to someone who has more control over the print outlet's website—if that person even exists.

But more often than not, a TV story will need to run on-air before it can run on the station's website. The exceptions are calendar listings for an event or run-of-the-mill announcements that the station may still want to recognize, without providing air-time to it.

Radio is a different beast. We rarely see radio interviews run online. In fact, many radio websites are rather pointless, which is one of the reasons we rarely pitch radio these days, opting to focus on podcasts. More on that in an upcoming chapter.

Non-Media Websites and Blogs

We do not consider traditional media websites as the only way to gain online coverage. Websites and blogs that aren't affiliated with the media can be just as important as media websites, if not more so.

However, online search engines will often place higher value on media websites than other types of websites. Therefore, getting placements in media websites may be worth more in a search engine's eyes than any other coverage you may secure.

That's not to say that some websites/blogs that aren't connected to the media can't bring great SEO value. So, it's worth understanding that you'd approach non-media affiliated websites pretty much the same way you'd approach traditional print/online media. Unless they're pay-to-play influencers, which we'll discuss in the social media chapter.

No matter the media, it is imperative to be polite and thoughtful with everyone, regardless of whether they're working out of a New York newsroom or their mother's dank basement. What is not thoughtful is sending mass emails without any thought as to what recipients might find useful. People who get coverage, no matter what type of outlet, do not spam others.

To avoid spamming, take notice of not only what a website covers, but *how* they cover it. For example, if a website never includes guest blog posts, don't ask them to include yours. Instead, see if they need a source to provide expertise on a topic that might interest them. Or better yet, build a relationship by connecting them with peers outside of your organization if they'd be better served that way. This thoughtful way of being is the essence of conducting professional PR.

PRINT DEADLINES

As I share information about deadlines for various print outlets, let me clarify what I mean by "deadline." From the PR point-of-view, there are two types of deadlines for media outreach:

1. When to start outreach.

2. The "drop-dead" deadline, after which outreach is too late.

Give attention to when to start outreach by factoring in a deadline that maximizes the opportunity for coverage. Effective outreach requires that you build in breathing room for some runaround time. For example, your contact could miss your first email or you have the wrong contact altogether. And even if you do have the right contact, you might need time to collect materials they request or handle other details.

However, we don't always come across PR-worthy opportunities with time to spare. That's why I provide some estimates about drop-dead timelines. If you have paid attention to deadlines, you will know when to go out on a limb with a late opportunity, and perhaps more importantly, when to let it go.

You also need to think about deadlines from the other side, which is after the newsworthy occurrence. We classify our press outreach into "before" and "after" stages:

- **"Before" stage**: When announcing something before it occurs, we're required to stay ahead of deadlines.

- **"After" stage**: When recapping something that already happened, we're offered more leeway. But don't delay outreach for too long or the media won't deem it as fresh anymore. For daily print outlets, it's fine to send updates one day after the occurrence. For non-daily print, or websites that don't have quick turnarounds, sending within one week is fine.

Not only are deadlines among different types of publications going to differ, the deadlines between two similar publications may be unique, with deadlines even varying among contacts at the same publication.

That's why it's important to get a strong handle on the unique intricacies of your media focus area, whether your focus is on location, topic or both. Make note of what you learn to build your efficiency and confidence in determining deadlines.

Let's review specific deadlines for different outlets and types of coverage.

Daily Newspapers

Daily newspapers typically focus on statewide news, or their particular region of the state, but may also include regional, national and international stories. Start initiating contact about three weeks ahead but consider three days ahead as your drop-dead deadline. Follow up in between, as deadlines approach.

Special Sections

Newspapers often publish weekly or annual special sections. For weekly inserts, contact them three weeks ahead. For annual sections, aim for three months ahead, with a rough drop-dead deadline of about six weeks prior.

Local/Community Newspapers

These papers cover neighborhood news and events. Their publishing frequency can vary from monthly, weekly or even a few times per week. Contact monthlies two months ahead and weeklies three weeks ahead, with an approximate final deadline of one or two weeks before publication.

Monthly City or Statewide Lifestyle Magazines

These magazines focus on entertainment and local features, with news that is about a month old. Aim to contact them three months ahead, with the drop-dead deadline usually being six weeks prior.

Quarterlies

Only released four times each year, quarterly publications focus on specific topics, such as wedding planning or regional travel. Therefore, they have way longer lead times, often six to eight months ahead.

Glossy Monthly Magazines

These magazines have a nationwide audience and are typically based in New York. Contact them six months ahead, but you may be okay to pitch five months prior.

Trade and Vertical Publications

Trade publications are specific to your industry, while verticals target specialized audiences. Start pitching these outlets three months ahead, but after understanding their deadlines, you may find that you're okay two months ahead.

Online Media or Non-Media Websites

Online media operates at such a fast pace, you almost have to predict the future rather than meet strict deadlines. While they can augment stories that have already been posted and morph coverage to fit current happenings, they're also working toward a specific mission, with feature articles that require planning.

Some may release editorial calendars, however you'll have to put your trend-spotting skills in action for those that don't. Study your online media targets to determine not just *what* they might cover, but *when*.

MORE ON WHO YOU'RE WORKING WITH

While I've introduced the roles of reporters and editors in print/online newsrooms, not only is there more to say about those roles, there are other roles to discuss as well. Here's an overview.

Editor

The editor holds a pivotal role in shaping a publication's content, overseeing everything from its broad editorial direction to the minutiae of individual sentence structure. While editors at larger outlets may not hand-select each story, they have the final say on most matters, from major editorial decisions down to what word is used in a sentence.

Reporter

Reporters are deeply entrenched in their specific beats, focusing on key stories within their assigned areas of interest. It's generally best to pitch story ideas directly to the reporter since the editor is not always assigning stories. However, cc'ing the editor on pitches can serve as a safeguard, because the editor can pass your idea on to other reporters if you started with the wrong contact.

Managing Editor

For larger publications, there's often a managing editor who oversees the newsroom's operations, while the editor focuses on other things.

When in doubt, I first go to the managing editor to ask who the best contact is for a particular story.

Editor-in-Chief / Editor-at-Large

At the top of the editorial hierarchy are roles like editor-in-chief and editor-at-large. Most likely, you wouldn't pitch the top editor in a large newsroom. But titles can sometimes be misleading. It's crucial to understand the publication's internal structure, because the editor-in-chief could be the only editor managing a newsroom of freelance reporters, in which case, they're your only contact.

Publisher

In the realm of publication ownership and management, the publisher reigns supreme. Responsible for the publication's overall financial success, the publisher ensures that advertising and subscription revenue exceed operating costs. Most of the time, they will not be your contact. Yet again, it's important to first investigate the size of the publication because the publisher could be the only person working for a small outfit, thus your only option.

Digital Editor

Finally, digital editors play a crucial role in transforming print content into digital formats. They decide what news should be placed on the website and where, while possibly also managing social media content. Include them on your pitch for online visibility and possibly for sharing on social media.

USE YOUR INSTINCTS

Navigating print and online media is as much about understanding deadlines as it is about knowing who to pitch. While there are general guidelines, each outlet operates on its own timeline, with its own titling hierarchy. The more you refine your approach—tracking patterns, anticipating needs and aligning with each publication's process—the better your results will be. The key is to balance this understanding with flexibility to ensure your outreach is timely, relevant and effective.

But pitching the right person at the right time is only part of the equation. Next, we'll delve into the nuances of broadcast and podcast media, where timing and storytelling take on an entirely different rhythm.

CHAPTER NINE

UNDERSTANDING RADIO AND PODCAST MEDIA

Here we will explore the nuanced strategies for securing coverage in the distinct platforms of radio and podcasts. While both mediums are audio-based, their differences in approach, organization and impact each necessitate tailored strategies.

We'll delve into the challenges of working with radio, including its stringent timing requirements and limited online presence, which diminish its SEO benefits. Consequently, few SEO opportunities often lessen the priority of securing radio coverage.

In contrast, podcasts offer a more accessible and potentially rewarding avenue for coverage. But the sheer volume of available podcasts demands a strategic approach to avoid becoming overwhelmed or misdirected.

Let's unravel these complexities to maximize your impact in the realm of audio.

HOW AND WHEN TO PITCH NEWS RADIO

The type of earned coverage you'll generally receive from radio will be from news stations rather than music and entertainment stations since the latter offer limited story-telling and news reporting opportunities. Typically, the same pitch you send to TV will work for radio, but you should replace any verbiage that references "visuals" with "sounds."

Rather than focusing on your pitch, it's sometimes more important to consider the strict timelines you'll need to abide by when pitching news radio. Here are the steps to take for garnering traditional news radio coverage, along with when to take those steps:

First, send your pitch to the newsroom (along with any reporters you may want to include) one day ahead of either: a) when you want the interview to be conducted, or b) when your event occurs.

Then, the following morning, call the newsroom to follow up on your pitch. It's imperative to call directly after the morning drive time window, which runs from about 6 to 9 a.m. Give them about five minutes to breathe after morning drive time ends before calling, but don't wait too much longer and risk bumping into their morning meeting or shift change.

The person who picks up the newsroom phone after drive time is either the person in charge (with the news director title, who may also be the reporter/anchor that's on-air during the shift) or is working very closely with them. Therefore, you can just go ahead and pitch/follow up with that person.

Ensure Spokespeople Are Available

Be ready for success in case the news station wants to interview someone right away. An immediate interview could be done via phone, aka "phoners," in which a call is recorded and aired later. Or, I suppose the call could be conducted live, but that might require some advance planning to ensure the timing is right for the station.

In fact, they may want to interview YOU right away. Don't do the interview if you aren't the spokesperson. Instead, you'll have to schedule a time for your spokesperson to call the radio contact—likely that same day.

There is nothing worse than pitching an interviewee and not being able to deliver. To avoid this, ensure your spokesperson is available around 9:15 a.m. to 2 p.m. on the day you're proactively pitching radio. Your interviewee doesn't need to block out that entire time frame, but they need to be relatively available.

If a radio station contacts you directly—asking for an interview on a topic or a source that you didn't pitch—you don't need to oblige with their schedule. However, hustling to meet their needs would increase the likelihood of a story coming to fruition, which is sometimes what PR is all about.

Pitching Events and Photo Ops

Another scenario is with an event, such as a 10 a.m. photo op. You can ask radio contacts to attend events, but their presence isn't imperative, because they can conduct a "phoner" with your spokesperson after the event. You'll likely have to call the station again after your event to get the phone interview scheduled, ideally for that afternoon around 12 - 3 p.m.

Radio Feature Stories

There is a difference between typical news and feature stories that require more planning. The FM music radio stations that mix thoughtful news coverage or local happenings into their routines will need to be approached differently.

I would reach out to these special types of shows or segments about three weeks before I want my interview to run, knowing I'd probably still be fine pitching about two weeks ahead. I'll likely have to follow up around two weeks ahead anyway and possibly even conduct a last attempt one week ahead.

RADIO TIMING RECAP

- One day before desired coverage date: Send pitch to the news desk email.

- Day of desired coverage date at 9:05 a.m.: Send email one more time, then immediately call to remind.

  » Hopefully, an interview will be set up. If not, move on.

  » If you really want the coverage, and/or you held a media event, call again after the event around 1 - 2 p.m., which is typically a slow time at the station.

- For special segments on entertainment or long-lead news shows, start contacting three weeks ahead, have plans firmed up one to two weeks ahead.

Also remember that no means no. Stop calling the station if they tell you they're not interested in running your story. Do not attempt to convince another contact at the station.

PEOPLE TO KNOW IN RADIO

Professional titles in radio differ depending on the type of station or show. Since most of you will likely focus on news radio shows first, let's start there.

Professional Titles at News Radio Stations

Radio newsrooms operate similarly to television newsrooms. Assignment desks not only receive pitches and tips, they also monitor news sources through tools like police scanners and social media.

However, in radio there's more mixing between roles. The person answering your call at the assignment desk might also be the on-air personality that reports on the story you've just sent over.

But if we were to put a label on them, they would go something like this:

Assignment editors, sometimes called **news directors** in radio, manage the assignment desk, handling incoming pitches, staying updated on current events and assigning stories to reporters.

That's not to say that radio **reporters** can't propose stories for coverage, but unlike radio hosts/anchors, they report from the field, sometimes providing live updates.

The radio **anchor/host** primarily works in the studio, hosting the entire show and connecting segments. You would rarely pitch an anchor as they are driving the entire ship. However, in small markets, the anchor might also be the reporter, who may also be the news director. This is why I just pitch whoever answers the news desk phone!

Professional Titles at FM or Entertainment Radio Stations

Some music radio stations weave current events into their programming, especially during morning drive time. If your story is music or entertainment related, it's more likely to run on entertainment radio stations, while your boring old B2B announcement may have little-to-no chance at all.

When pitching entertainment or music radio stations, here are the roles to pay attention to:

Hosts/DJs (or anchors) are the on-air voices. In smaller stations, they might also be the news directors, if there is a news component to the station. With budget cuts, many hosts take on multiple roles. Interviews are shorter or nonexistent, which means the hosts could share your news without interviewing anyone.

The other roles you may need to know about include promotion and program directors. **Promotion directors** handle creative partnerships, like giveaways and on-air contests, to boost brand exposure. While **program directors** are the go-to for music pitches.

DIGITAL HURDLES IN RADIO

For those that value an online presence, it's important to note that the radio stories we generate don't seem to easily end up online, therefore the SEO value from radio is minimal to non-existent.

In fact, websites for radio stations are just plain odd. They almost appear to be rebroadcasting centers and not necessarily where they post links or keywords that would point back to your website to boost your SEO. The exceptions can be large stations like National Public Radio (NPR) because they have substantial websites, but stories on those are much harder to come by.

For these reasons, along with the strict timing particulars, we rarely focus our efforts on radio anymore, opting to skip ahead to the next generation of audio—podcasts.

PODCASTS: THE NEW RADIO

Podcasting has recently exploded in popularity. There were more than 4.4 million podcasts worldwide in March of 2025.[*] What's more compelling is data indicating that podcast hosts are not merely speaking into the void. For the first time in America, on-demand audio received more ear-time than radio in 2023, according to Edison Research. They also showed that 47% of U.S. residents listened to podcasts on a monthly basis in 2024 and 34% listened weekly.[†]

---

[*]   "Total Podcasts in the Index," Podcast Index, accessed March 4, 2025, at https://podcastindex.org/.

[†]   "Weekly Insights 8.23.2023 On-Demand Audio Passes Linear Audio," Edison Research, accessed March 4, 2025, at https://www.edisonresearch.com/weekly-insights-8-23-2023-on-demand-audio-passes-linear-audio/.

Pitching Podcasts

The process for pitching podcasts can be similar to pitching other forms of media. As always, start with a succinct pitch that incorporates why your expert would be an ideal guest, and importantly, what topics they can discuss in an episode.

In terms of who to pitch, hopefully the podcast's website will give you an idea of who you're supposed to contact with ideas—whether it's the host, producer or someone else with the organization. The website may also require you to fill out a form for guest proposals.

Media Podcasts

There is a distinction between regular podcasts and those produced by traditional media, the latter of which typically dig deeper into news they already covered in their original medium. They do this by dialoguing with each other about previous stories or rebroadcasting radio segments into podcast format.

That's why it might be best to approach media podcasts by first seeking placements within their traditional formats (print, blog, radio or TV). And if they recognize how the resulting coverage could be expanded upon in the podcast, they might funnel you there.

Sometimes media outlets will produce targeted podcasts on a niche topic, such as the environment or entertainment. So, it might be worthwhile to understand what podcast opportunities exist among your media targets, especially if you can't place an eccentric story in traditional formats.

Podcast Deadlines

While deadlines for podcasts can be nebulous, we still need to bring some sort of structure to the process. Do this by uncovering roughly how often and when episodes are being released from your targeted podcasts. Compare this schedule against what you'd like to feature on the podcasts to create your own deadlines. For example, a product promotion may have an expiration date, or a guest can only offer insight related to a specific season.

Pad your time accordingly and don't forget to add important dates in your marketing/content calendar.

CAPTURING A UNIQUE AUDIENCE

After understanding the nuances surrounding podcasts, you may be wondering if they're worth the effort. GWI Consumer Research summarized the audience podcasts are attracting.*

"Listeners of podcasts are much more inquisitive and ahead of the tech adoption curve. Heavier podcast listeners are more receptive to ads promoting diversity and raising social awareness than their radio-listening counterparts. They're more likely to consider themselves opinion leaders, think immigration is good for their country, and say that contributing to their community is important to them."

Keeping that in mind, your organization may benefit from the extra work required to capture the engaged audience of podcast listeners.

---

* GWI, "The Global Media Landscape."

CHAPTER TEN

UNDERSTANDING TELEVISION MEDIA

Television news works in such a particular way that I've launched into this chapter by offering a set of rules that will help you work effectively with any type of media, but especially TV. While some of these rules focus on how to conduct yourself on the phone, you'll hardly ever have to call other types of media besides TV. But for TV, you'll be hard-pressed to land any type of story if you don't call to follow up on your pitch.

Therefore, keep the following media etiquette rules in mind when starting out:

- Rule 1: Never launch into a phone pitch without asking if the person on the other end has time to hear you out.

- Rule 2: Make your personal introduction brief. You'll lose them if you recite a long company name and title.

  Combine rules one and two by incorporating your pitch into your introduction, then pause to ask if they have a moment, like:

"Hi, this is [first name only] calling about the [brief thing you're calling about, may not even include name of your organization]. Do you have a second?:

- Rule 3: Do what they ask of you, whether that's calling them back at a certain time or scrounging up more information.

- Rule 4: Deliver on your promises. Find out who's around to represent your organization before offering interviews.

- Rule 5: Be easy to reach after sending out news. Place your contact information in the communication and always keep your phone with you and on.

- Rule 6: Never follow up more than two times on the exact same pitch to the exact same contact.

Let's put these rules in action through the following example:

Your new store, Urban Haven Boutique, is having its ribbon cutting today. You've enhanced the boring old ribbon cutting event by hosting 12 students from the local art school to unveil their fashion designs at the event.

The students will be at the ribbon cutting to display their work, while the store's unique features, like limited edition collections, interactive displays and customization stations, will be highlighted.

After sending an email or media advisory inviting the media to attend, you'll want to call to follow up on it. This could be the most important part of the campaign.

Here's how you'll start this pitch: "This is Sally calling about the fashion design unveiling happening today with the 12 local art school students. Do you have a second?"

Note the following key elements:

First Element

"Sally." This is as much of an introduction as is needed. In fact, this is an unnecessary formality that can go away, but sometimes it's done by habit or can provide a mental warm up.

Second Element

"Fashion design unveiling with the 12 local art school students." This is your pitch. That's it. You don't need to include the store's name because nobody cares (yet). The point is to get their attention by swiftly summarizing what's going to happen. The following parts help seal the deal:

- The number of students in attendance as the media loves numbers.

- The word "unveiling" sums up that this is a visual event.

- Since students are typically kids, and the media loves kids, animals and charities, you really can't go wrong here.

I didn't include anything about the new boutique opening or ribbon cutting because my goal is to have TV stations attend the event. Stores open and ribbons are cut every day, so I don't need to spend precious time losing TV over uninteresting details that are already in the media pitch/advisory.

Third Element

"Do you have a second?" A sort of fumbling awkwardness typically occurs next, with them either saying they only have a minute or they begin searching for the email. However, this pause allows them to recall what was sent or realize they may be missing out.

If they are physically or mentally searching during this pause, you can casually remind them when the event is, offer more details and possibly resend your pitch while they're on the phone. Hopefully, it bubbles to the top of their inbox while you've got them on the phone so you can be sure they received it. They might even offer their intentions to cover it or not.

BEST WAY TO GET TV: PHOTO OPPORTUNITIES

Most TV coverage isn't gained by booking an on-air slot with an anchor. Rather, a field reporter and/or "camera" (short for camera person) visits a location to cover a story. The best way to obtain this type of coverage is to create something like what I previously described.

I call these mini media events "photo opportunities" (photo ops). They are special moments in time for the media to "capture." While they will work for other types of media, they're often a necessity for garnering local TV news coverage.

Examples of Photo Opportunities Include:

- Groundbreaking for new construction

- Ribbon cutting for new office/location*

- Oversized check presentation*

- Public art unveiling

- Art installation

- Special performance for children

- The measuring of a race course (run, walk or bike event)

---

* Add more to it: incorporate other important things. Talking heads—such as politicians, VIPs, donors—are good but visually thin. What can your photo op players literally DO?

- Large scale event set up/move-in

- New building/structure tours

- Moving days for notable organizations

- Volunteering or doing something active in the community

- The event itself (along with, or instead of, a pre-event photo op)

- Large-scale donation of food, clothing or other physical item drop off

- Any other thing that you can make visual or active

TIMING IS EVERYTHING

The best timing for photo opportunities, and other media events, is **10 a.m. during weekdays.**

Your 10 a.m. event will occur directly after the **"morning meeting"** that happens at most TV news stations around 9 a.m. when the day's stories are selected. With their assignments in-hand, the camera people and reporters scramble out after the meeting on a quest to cover their assigned stories.

Calling right before their 9 a.m. meeting reminds them to discuss your story. Hosting the event at 10 a.m. lessens the chances they're called off to a breaking news story. Moreover, the 10 a.m. timing provides an excellent window for the station to air the footage on all newscasts, beginning at 12 noon, running through the 4 p.m., 5 p.m. and 6 p.m. time slots and into the evening news. Yes, it is possible for the very same story to run on all these newscasts.

When promoting a public event, you can create a photo op to ensure media coverage runs before the public event date. However, you'll want to get an event calendar listing out well in advance, sending it to all types of newsrooms, including TV news desks, so they can incorporate it into their websites or discuss it on-air.

WHERE TO SEND AND WHO TO CALL

Send photo op news to the email address designated for the "**assignment desk**," or general news email. Your email should be received by the "**assignment editor**," or those working on "the desk." They are sometimes called content editors, but everyone will know what you mean if you ask for the assignment editor or assignment desk.

With an ear on the police scanners (what the police are saying to each other), an eye on social media and another on the newsroom's constantly overflowing inbox, these are the people that will do the following with your story:

1. Put it in "the file" to be discussed at the next news meeting

2. Send it to a reporter who may be interested

3. Delete it

4. Ignore it

Don't let #4 happen. Call the desk to ensure they received your story idea. You don't even have to ask for the assignment editor. Whoever answers can file your story away for discussion later.

Most times, my firm will repeat the send/call cycle twice—sending the pitch in the afternoon (one day before the photo op) and calling around 2 p.m. (ahead of their news shows) to ensure they received it (resending if they didn't receive it). Then, we'll send it an additional time the next morning before the 9 a.m. news meeting, calling once again immediately after sending it to remind them of the photo op.

If you're feeling that this is overkill, it's fine to send your photo op pitch one day before it occurs and then call only on the day of the photo op. Calling the morning of your news occurrence is not optional—it is imperative.

BE YOUR OWN NEWSROOM

Once your photo op is underway, don't be disappointed if some (or none!) of the TV stations attend. If your event is visual and you've followed all outreach steps, what ends up happening is almost up to fate. You could hit a home run during a slow news day, but on a day fraught with breaking news, you may not be able to get anyone out.

If the latter is the case, pull out your smartphone and do the TV station's job for them. They'll run photos and videos taken by community members. However, **you must send photos/videos to assignment desks by 2 p.m. (at the latest!) on the day of the event** so you don't bump against their news deadlines. Then, call the assignment desk right after sending photos/video to ensure they were received.

Photo/Video Guidelines for TV

Shoot horizontal photos/videos for TV. The photos don't need to be smiling groups of people posing for the camera. A handful of candid action shots of what happened at the event are better.

The video format that's needed for TV is called B-roll. "Voiced over" by the anchor back at the station, B-roll captures the scene of the event through movement and action. There's no need to film your own interviews for the station, just send them a handful of 10 to 30 second B-roll videos that span left to right showing the action.

In your post-event email, include a link to a shared Dropbox or Google Drive folder that houses your neatly organized photos/videos. Don't overload the folder with junk. Delete unusable and duplicate images, while labeling each file with your organization's name and event.

OTHER TV OPPORTUNITIES

Zoom Interviews

When Zoom exploded during the coronavirus pandemic, it worked its way into TV news as well. No longer did we need to go into the studio or meet a camera person somewhere to conduct an interview.

The technology for off-site interviews was available before the pandemic, but when the only option for interviews became digital, TV stations were forced to use platforms like Zoom. Of course, some TV stations like to make life hard on us by using their preferred digital recording device, which isn't always Zoom.

Zoom interviews are landed the same way in-person interviews are landed, with the same timing and news hook particulars. What's different is that these platforms have opened the world up to regular people. Now we can conduct national and even international TV interviews from the comfort of our own homes.

Evening Shift TV Change

An evening shift change typically occurs between 2 to 3 p.m., led by an additional news meeting to discuss what the nighttime shift will cover. If you must promote a nighttime event, you'll still want to get on the radar of the morning shift. But ask when the nighttime assignment editor arrives and when their news meeting is so you know when to follow up.

I would refrain from organizing a media event occurring in the afternoon or evening because they have less staff on hand and the day shift has more pull. But you may be stuck with a previously arranged event or a compelling public event that you might as well invite nighttime cameras to.

You can still send photos/video of such events to newsrooms, even after the 2 p.m. photo/video deadline because that timing doesn't apply for events falling after the day shift's window. Your materials can run on the evening news or early the next morning.

Weekend TV News

Enlist a monitoring service to tell you which stations run your coverage and when. If your photo op was during a weekday, and the monitoring service shows it didn't run, your opportunity to get it to run the following day is probably shot.

Unless your photo op was on a Friday. While it might be hard for press to show up to your event, it could be a prime opportunity for the weekend shift to run the footage you took during Friday's event.

As far as press outreach, follow all the same steps on Friday, but then on Saturday morning call the stations that didn't run it. A different crew could be working on Saturday, therefore your phone calls could be newly received.

Or you may be stuck with a weekend photo op. Follow the same steps, including timing details, for weekend events. Taking your own photos and video may be important because newsroom staff is slimmer on weekends, lessening the chances they'll attend your event. Unlike during the week, the station may consider running footage from a Saturday event on the following day, Sunday.

Morning Shows

Booking a morning show most likely means that you've booked a features reporter to spend the early morning hours with you at a designated location as they broadcast live segments that cut into the news being filmed back at the station.

Most morning show feature reporters schedule and manage their own segments. Start pitching them about six weeks in advance, but the typical deadline to secure them is about four weeks in advance.

Watch the reporter's usual coverage to tailor your pitch to their style. Also, look for the typical number of segments they're assigned each morning and how long each segment is. Use this information in your pitch to sketch out a brief timeline of your proposed segments. This allows you to demonstrate your "producer" chops.

While TV shows have producers that organize everything, features reporters rarely have their own producers dedicated to organizing their on-air time. Serving in a producer capacity will prove invaluable to the reporter, likely leading to a long-term relationship with more bookings.

Once you get a commitment, ask the reporter for their "rundown," which includes the time and length of each live segment so you can help the reporter book interviewees and/or segment ideas. Some reporters are fine with a few "talking heads," while some are not. The only way to find out is to run your ideas by the reporter before you start working too hard on prepping and lining people up.

Type up your rundown in order of segments, including:

- The time each segment is slated to go live.

- Padding time of when the interviewee will arrive on-site.

  » Always have interviewees arrive one half hour before their live segment.

- Each interviewee's name, cell phone number and what they will talk about/do on-air.

Interviewees might have to partake in an activity while being interviewed to turn a talking head into a visual TV story. Or the interviewee could talk while the reporter is doing something active. Think about TV as you may have been told to write—show rather than tell. For example, chefs don't just stand there and talk on TV, they work with food *while* talking about it.

How to turn a "talking head" into a "moving body":

- Have the interviewee teach the reporter how to do something.

- Have the interviewee tour, show or demonstrate the thing they are talking about.

- Have the reporter and interviewee contribute to an effort that's being talked about, such as building a house during a segment featuring Habitat for Humanity.

- Provide pictures and video to the station ahead of time that can air during the interview.

Days in advance, we get on the phone with each morning show interviewee to ensure they can handle themselves on TV. We explain what will happen during their designated time slot and what their role is, sometimes incorporating any ideas they may have, while constantly reiterating that live TV is fun and casual to set them at ease. We'll also offer a few **TV pointers** in a nonchalant manner (so we don't make them nervous), including:

- Don't look at the camera. They will stick it in your face and you'll think you are supposed to look at it, but you are supposed to have a conversation with the reporter.

  » If you accidentally glance at the camera, don't worry about it and move the conversation forward.

- Don't wear white or busy, patterned shirts.

- Turn your cell phone off (remind everyone before the cameras start rolling).

- Relax and smile! Remember, this is fun!

ADDITIONAL TV MEDIA CONTACTS

While most morning show features reporters do not have dedicated producers, most TV shows have **producers** running the entire show. Shielded by the assignment desk/editor, gaining access to producers can be difficult. But on typical straightforward news shows in local markets, you'll rely on the assignment editor, and the producer simply puts it all together. However, you may want to seek out the producer for entertainment-focused shows or special shows that run at odd times to find out if these are the type of producers that can be pitched.

Sometimes, there are **digital producers** at TV stations who decide which stories make it onto the website or social media. Not all stories that air on TV make it online, just as not all online stories make it on TV. In some instances, the latter concept works out just great, especially if SEO is your aim.

Also, you may be wondering when you might pitch a TV **reporter** directly. You'd loop them into anything sent to the assignment desk/ newsroom if your topic fits with one of their beats, such as: health, business/finance, education, consumer protection and the environment. If your story idea directly relates to their coverage area, you might try this person first (as opposed to it being assigned by "the desk") because they may create a more in-depth story and share it with their followers.

PURCHASED TV COVERAGE

It's worth mentioning that some of the lighthearted segments that run in the news program's lineup have been purchased, especially news from morning show features reporters. You may even stumble across an entire "news" program that only highlights advertising content. The guests, products and services being featured may look like news stories, but have actually paid for the recognition.

These types of shows typically run after the morning news, between 9 a.m. to 11 a.m. Of course, the better shows feature more than just paid content, providing a mix of entertaining or helpful feature stories, alongside purchased stories.

When an idea to purchase TV news coverage surfaces, the PR team or department should be involved. Not only can PR people provide advice about whether there may be opportunities for free coverage, someone will have to work with the news department to help secure live-shot locations, organize rundowns, build relationships and more.

TV TIMING RECAP

Here is a recap of the timing suggestions I noted throughout, since timing and reminding are the key to success with TV!

- One day before the desired coverage date: Send pitch to the news desk email.

- One day before desired coverage date, before 2 p.m.: Call to follow up after sending the pitch to ensure they received it.

  » Try to make sure it's "in the file" for discussion at the next morning meeting.

- Day of desired coverage date, before 9 a.m.: Send email one more time and immediately call to remind them of the event and ensure they have the pitch.

- Day of desired coverage date, before 2 p.m.: Send photos/video from the event to those that couldn't make it. Call immediately after sending to ensure they have the photos/videos.

- For morning show reporters, start contacting six weeks ahead, have plans firmed up four weeks ahead.

Finally, remember "no" means no. Stop calling the station if they tell you they're not interested in running your story. Do not attempt to convince another contact at the station.

CHAPTER ELEVEN

ADDING SOCIAL MEDIA TO PR

After the first book in this series was published, it seemed that the only question I received from readers pertained to using social media in relation to PR. I've always been a little stumped by this question, wondering if I was missing the efficiency that social media surely provided PR.

In short, I haven't found social media to be a great way to connect with journalists. Whenever I have succeeded in making contact through social media, the journalist will inevitably ask me to email more information. That's why I take the opposite approach, which is to email journalists first and then ping them on social if I don't hear back.

Of course, if you've worked with a journalist for a while and know that social media is the best way to reach them, then go that route. But I can hardly remember a time that this was true, except perhaps before Twitter became X, and that seemed to be very specific to tech reporters.

Regardless, the type of people who want to use social media as a PR shortcut aren't particularly enthusiastic to hear how social media *adds to*, not *cuts out*, PR work. But since you've gotten this far within these pages, you are not one of those people. You want to know how to maximize your work. And you probably understand that it takes more than minimal effort to produce better results. So, the tips on how to use social media to enhance (not reduce!) your PR work are for you.

STEP ONE: PLACE ORIGINAL NEWS COVERAGE

People are still paying attention to the news, they simply find it through intermediaries like social media. But if you're thinking you can skip the step of getting your story published in the original news medium, and go straight to their social channels—think again. It's rare for an outlet to run news on their social media channels before, or instead of, their original mediums first.

Social media managers at news outlets typically weed through stories their outlets have already published to decide what they'll share on social. Regardless, why wouldn't you want to get the story first published on the original news medium before it hits social media? Not only would that method bring more eyeballs to the story, it would add more to your website's SEO.

Therefore, the first step for using social media to enhance your PR efforts is to garner coverage on original news mediums, such as in the actual newspaper, magazine, website, podcast, TV or radio station.

STEP TWO: PLACE COVERAGE ON NEWS OUTLETS' SOCIAL MEDIA

If your story runs in an original news medium, but doesn't appear on that medium's social platforms, nudge the social manager to see if they'll run it for you. Just know that most news organizations have guidelines about what they can share on social media, such as the story's impact, release date, website engagement, etc.

If you have trouble finding the social media manager on the editorial roster, look for them in the marketing, management or digital departments. Incidentally, the social media manager seems like the type of person that may be more receptive to receiving a pitch through social media.

STEP THREE: PLACE COVERAGE ON YOUR OWN SOCIAL CHANNELS

With people finding news through social media, the control is back in our hands. You don't need to rely on audiences tuning in to a news program or picking up the newspaper to see your news story. Take charge by posting coverage that you've earned on your social channels. Put dollars behind these posts to increase visibility even more.

But first, the 2024 Digital News Report* (mentioned in the introduction) has an invaluable tool that can help you understand where your audiences are spending time. After clicking the "Interactive" button on the report, you can break down data by country, age group, gender, etc. — and search by topics like popular social networks, what brands are trusted, who's paying for digital news, who's listening to podcasts, who's avoiding news and more.

While you can use the tool to learn more about what relates to your needs, here's how the tool depicted 2024 social media usage in the U.S. for all age groups (18 to over 55 years old):

- 61% used Facebook for any reason, 31% for news.

- 60% used YouTube for any reason, 29% for news.

- 36% used Instagram for any reason, 14% for news.

---

* Reuters Institute, "Digital News Report 2024."

- 25% used X (formerly Twitter) for any reason, 15% for news.

- 23% used TikTok for any reason, 9% for news.

When breaking these stats down by age group, YouTube appears to be the most used platform from age 18 clear through to age 54! Instagram follows as the second most used platform for 18 - 34 year olds, with Facebook coming in third place for this group. Moving up the age scale, Facebook shifts into second place ahead of Instagram for 35 - 54 year olds. While the 55 and over set rely on Facebook as their first go-to, with YouTube coming in second, followed by Instagram.

It's worth continuing to examine where your audiences are spending time on social media. New platforms are often released and fickle consumers easily change their ways. Taking time to either research or test your assumptions on social media becomes increasingly important if you'll be spending money on any of the platforms.

ADVERTISING ON SOCIAL MEDIA

Advertising on social media transforms you into a stealthy ninja because of how granularly you can target audiences—from demographics and locations to interests, behaviors and more! While traditional ads can run on social media, you can also "sponsor" or "boost" social media posts.

Even though advertising on Facebook and Instagram is purchased and managed through Meta, the targeting capabilities between the platforms vary slightly. For instance, Facebook provides extra ways of targeting through education, relationship status and job title, along with zip code and hobbies. Whereas Instagram only offers the more general targeting that Facebook also provides, such as age, gender, region, city and interests. We're not sure what Meta's Threads will bring as targeted advertising is now being tested on the platform as I am writing this in early 2025.

X, TikTok and YouTube offer the same type of targeting options as Instagram, although YouTube has an extra "parental status" option.

Understandably, LinkedIn provides more professional ways of targeting, such as job title, industry, company size, skills, degrees and years of experience.

The platforms also have their own ways of allowing you to build unique targeting lists with your own information (such as website visitors and customer lists). Called "lookalike" or "matched" audiences, you can reach new people that are similar to your existing followers, website visitors, customer lists, etc.

Targeting Journalists Through Social Media Advertising

You can also use social media advertising to prime journalists for a pitch that's about to come, or to remind them of the importance of a pitch that's already been sent. Target journalists through zip code (to help reach local news) and job title (only on Facebook and LinkedIn), or "interests" (to match up with reporter beats). For example, education would likely show up as an interest for an education reporter, whereas science might show up as an interest for a science reporter.

I wouldn't spend money trying to blast journalists with senseless advertisements. Boost posts that convey how urgent or interesting a particular topic is. For example, the boosted post could link to a news article that covers the topic in a different way than you're pitching. You can add your unique thoughts, which may be your pitch angle, in the post that shares the article.

Let me state for the record that I don't think this is a replacement for traditional PR—it's just an interesting way to add more depth to a compelling PR campaign.

MAXIMIZING JOURNALIST ENGAGEMENT ON SOCIAL MEDIA

Meaningfully engaging with journalists who are active on social media is likely more impactful than trying to target them through social advertising. Commenting on their posts helps them in more ways than you know. In today's world, where journalists must be everywhere all at once, they also need to drum up social media interest for the stories they produce.

Go beyond telling journalists that you like their work when they post it on social media. Tell them *what* you liked, or what you agreed with, to provide some meat to your comment. Perhaps this will entice other people to dialogue within the post, furthering visibility for the journalist and their story. But don't think too hard about this. Try to directly engage as best you can.

RESEARCHING JOURNALISTS, OUTLETS AND STORY IDEAS ON SOCIAL MEDIA

Just as you turn to search engines to research journalists, outlets and story ideas, social media can add nuance and efficiency to the process. You can track key phrases and trends on LinkedIn and X, join industry-specific groups on Facebook and track relevant hashtags on Instagram, X, LinkedIn and Facebook—all for free.

However, it may be easier to do this with a social media monitoring tool—like Hootsuite, Sprout Social, BuzzSumo or Brandwatch—which may also provide better results. I like being able to organize each topic within its own dedicated column or area. Otherwise, my mind is hopping from topic-to-topic, client-to-client.

While Hootsuite and Sprout Social offer limited free plans for basic alerts, you may have to pay for deeper services. The fees are typically modest and can offer additional help with scheduling, posting and more. But if you're using a media database, like Meltwater or Cision, you may want to see if your service includes social media monitoring functions.

After gathering information through social media monitoring, attempt to analyze your findings. I typically go by instinct here, with one post sparking an idea, another providing a follow up angle and another tipping me off to a new media contact. But if you want to get granular about it, tools like BuzzSumo can help you understand trending topics, along with how content is performing, allowing you to adapt your PR strategies accordingly.

WORKING WITH SOCIAL MEDIA INFLUENCERS

I would be remiss to write a chapter about social media and exclude a section on how to work with social media influencers. To be honest, my firm doesn't have a lot of experience in this arena since we work with mostly B2B companies or organizations like schools, foundations and credit unions.

However, a savvy marketer would note that influencers exist in all arenas. For example, a school might ask current families to speak about their positive experiences with prospective families. Or a B2B organization might rely on referrals from industry thought leaders to solicit new customers. These are all ways to leverage influencers.

But when people ask about influencer marketing, they're wondering about the popular TikTok mom who sneaks product mentions into her skits, or the traveling YouTube diva who slides hotel reviews into her podcast, or the Instagram doctor who includes supplement recommendations into her talks.

These types of influencers are typically recommending other people's products and services for a fee or trade. Experts say the best way to work with them is to set a predetermined budget (whether in the form of cash or trade), approach them with your partnership idea and then get ready to negotiate.

Apparently, it is very customary for influencers to negotiate offers, resulting in miscellaneous contract changes that need to be managed by a detail-oriented person. Also, influencers are content creators, so don't be surprised if they place guidelines around your demands, while creatively building upon your ideas. Understanding how they work will help you launch into a mutually successful partnership.

Let me direct you to the following resources to learn more about influencer marketing. The thought leader who puts a different perspective on it is Jason Falls of Winfluence. Influencer Marketing Hub offers a lot of resources, while a tool like Later, which is a social media marketing tool with an influencer marketing platform, can help you find, engage and manage influencers.

AMPLIFY YOUR REACH:
THE SYNERGY OF PR AND SOCIAL MEDIA

The real value of social media lies within its ability to complement traditional PR methods by offering opportunities to place stories in front of a larger portion of the public. This increased visibility not only enhances reach, but also provides us with more control over the dissemination of our work.

Ultimately, social media is an extension of the traditional PR toolkit. It adds layers of engagement and visibility, but does not replace the foundational work of PR planning, pitching and following up. Embrace the potential of social media, but remember to use it as a part of a well-rounded PR strategy, leveraging its strengths to maximize your reach and impact.

CHAPTER TWELVE

COMBINING SEARCH ENGINE OPTIMIZATION AND PR

The similarities between organic search engine optimization (SEO) and earned media cannot be denied. Organic SEO improves a website's ranking in search engines through natural methods that are not based on payment to search engines, just as earned media uses free methods to increase visibility.

The two disciplines work hand-in-hand when taking PR online. Not only do most media outlets have an online presence, some are only online. So even if you're practicing PR without a thought about SEO, you'll likely increase your SEO by happenstance.

But it's time to take SEO-driven PR to the next level. We've already explored how content fuels organic SEO, now we'll focus on other ways of increasing SEO, which include how the website is structured and how to obtain links and/or mentions from other websites.

Let's dive into how the most efficient teams combine SEO and PR to build lasting impact.

HOW THE WEBSITE IS BUILT

First, it's imperative that new websites are built in an "SEO-friendly" way because this is something that laypeople, such as a PR person like myself, can't come back and fix later. Sure, laypeople can push out quality content and obtain credible links from other websites, but these attempts won't be as effective if the website is poorly structured. That's why when you're launching a new website, it's important to find a web developer that understands SEO.

For an existing website, find out what platform it was built on to see if you're on the right track. High quality platforms like WordPress were made to help websites perform well in search. But even WordPress sites aren't perfect, so you may want to have websites that appear to be in good shape evaluated nonetheless.

How to Check Your Website's Rank

A quick way to check your website's rank with search engines is to sign up for a free version of SEO software like Moz, Semrush or Ahrefs. If you download the Moz plug-in to your Chrome browser, a little box in the upper-right corner of the Chrome interface will list the Domain Authority of any website you're on, as long as you're signed in to Moz.

Created by Moz, Domain Authority (DA) is a type of measurement that attempts to communicate how well a website performs in search engines. The scale is 1 - 100, with 1 being the lowest end of the scale and 100 being the highest. To give you an idea, *The New York Times'* homepage holds a DA of 95 and *The Wall Street Journal's* DA is 94. The *Portland Business Journal* ranks at 92 and *The Oregonian* ranks at 87, while your hometown newspapers are likely similar. Other websites that rank high are colleges and healthcare organizations (likely around 50 - 80 DA range).

Since SEO is so important to our clients, we use DA as a measurement to understand which online publications we should pitch, moving us into the other way of increasing SEO: obtaining links (and mentions) from other websites to build a "backlink" profile.

OBTAINING LINKS AND MENTIONS

When another website links to your website, it's known as "backlinking," or sometimes just "linking." Backlinks/links send signals to search engines, essentially helping them find and rank websites. They have been so important to SEO that many websites attempt to pay for them. However, Google can ignore paid links or even demote websites that engage in spammy practices—like keyword stuffing and exorbitant link buying—in the search engine results pages (SERPs).

For reasons like these, the average Joe believes it's very important to obtain links for free. However, SEO circles are debating whether links are still important. Might obtaining a mere mention of your brand or keyword (without the link) from another website suffice?

"Over time, the weight on the links at some point will drop off a little bit as we can figure out a little bit better how the content fits in within the context of the whole web," John Mueller, Senior Search Analysis, Google.*

With Google finding new ways to rank websites that do not include evaluating backlinks, we can rest a little easier. After all, some media websites have policies against including links in their stories. Moreover, it has been said that earning a mention from a quality website still helps SEO, maybe not as much as if it included a link, but we can only control so much.

However, if you land a story in a publication that *does* include links, don't look the other way if they failed to include a link in your story.

---

* "Is Link Building Still Relevant to SEO in 2023?," SEER Interactive, accessed March 9, 2025 at https://www.seerinteractive.com/insights/is-link-building-still-relevant#:~:text=In%20short%2C%20yes%2C%20link%20building,over%20quality%20are%20long%20over.

Politely approach your contact by first thanking them for the story, then ask if they wouldn't mind adding a link back to your website. Of course, end with the obligatory "don't worry about it if it's not possible."

I wouldn't necessarily bug them about this more than once. You took all the appropriate steps and a mention is good enough!

Nofollow Versus Follow Links

Another debate surrounds the type of link that a website might provide to another. Links are categorized as "follow" by default, which means that search engines will recognize them. Conversely, a link can be manually set as no-follow ("nofollow") to avoid passing signals to search engines.

A lot of media websites set their links to nofollow — if they even give links at all — to maintain their neutral status. We used to avoid pitching websites that gave nofollow links. Or we would ask *approachable* media outlets to change nofollow links to follow links. But the technicalities make this a larger request than just asking for a link. And with Google finding new ways to rank websites, some may wonder if this is a petty request.

However, if you could only choose one earned media opportunity where all things are equal, except for the type of link they give, you'd choose the opportunity that provides the follow link.

STEPS TO INFUSE TRADITIONAL PR WITH SEO

Let's recap what we've learned so far, with some additional thoughts to create a list of steps to follow when attempting to bring SEO into your PR efforts. The most important and first step is to incorporate some type of website measurement data into your media lists. As mentioned, we rely on DA.

Media websites with higher DAs would generally be viewed as more important than those with lower DAs. But it isn't always that easy. Here are other questions to ask when prioritizing websites:

- Does the website give links? If not, does this matter?

- Are the links nofollow or follow? Again, does it matter?

- How easy is it to get included in the website? For example, do all the stories that make it into the traditional platform, such as a newspaper, automatically get placed online?

- Other marketing considerations:

  » Will this website reach your demographic?

  » Does it share published stories on social media?

  » Does it offer other opportunities, such as podcast interviews or a blurb in their traditional medium?

Once your list reflects your priorities, PR outreach that has an SEO focus won't look too different than traditional PR.

If you've already sent your pitch to the beat reporter, editor or producer, you may decide to follow up with the digital news editor. Sometimes, you will 'cc all the pertinent contacts at one media outlet, including the digital news editor, and see what happens. Maybe by doing this, the story will only end up online and you'll be happy with this.

If the story is only placed in the traditional medium, you might want to contact the digital news editor (or whoever oversees the website) to inquire if they'll also include the story online. You could ask if they need anything different (like slightly augmented copy or a specific link) to grant your request.

OTHER SEO CONUNDRUMS

Only focusing on the top ways to increase SEO would be missing the point. SEO is so important to marketing and PR, that we're constantly uncovering new questions that help refine our strategies over time. Here are some common themes that we frequently run across and how we approach them.

SEO Implications of Advertorials

Purchasing an advertorial from a reputable media website is quite different from purchasing a link from a spammy website. But even still, you'll want to make sure the website you're considering doing business with performs well in search engines. This means looking beyond just the website's DA.

An SEO expert once remarked, "This website has a DA of 52, but it behaves like a 22 in the SERPs." What? Upon further inquiry, I learned that Moz attributes every link that a website has to its overall DA, even if some of those links aren't recognized by search engines. Remember, DA is a metric for mere humans to gauge whether search engines think a website is valuable. There's no way to fully understand how the algorithms truly work.

However, Moz can help you dig beyond DA. Paste the website's URL into Moz's Link Research/Link Explorer section to view the website's backlinks (by clicking in-bound links). If you find many 404s, errors or shortened links (like bit.ly), understand that Google might not recognize them as significant for ranking.

If this feels too complex, trust your instincts. Be cautious of websites that:

- Post articles on themes that don't mix, like health, cars, cooking, finance, current events and culture all in one place.

- Haven't posted in years or still display posts from two years ago on their homepage.

- Feature outdated mastheads, odd hero images (the top image on the homepage) or logos that seem unprofessional.

These are signs of a low-quality site offering cheap visibility that you should avoid because your search results could be damaged by association with certain websites. Even if a site appears to have a good DA, consider if you'd visit it or take it seriously as a member of your target audience.

If a website passes these checks, consider placing an advertorial if:

- You've exhausted all PR steps and can't get a quality bylined article placed.

- You need to reach a very specific audience.

- Your topic is crucial and needs more exposure.

It's important to note that advertorials labeled as "sponsored" or "paid" may be ignored by search engines—even if the advertorial is on a quality website. But at least your search ranking will not be damaged when purchasing through a quality website. However, this only matters if SEO is your sole focus. Ideally, you're thinking more holistically, as the article could still drive traffic, support a call-to-action (CTA), build credibility and more.

Paying for sponsored articles is the kind of paid media strategy that PR and SEO purists can get involved in. PR skills are needed to develop the topic, create the piece and target the right audience. SEO strategies are essential for evaluating the benefits (or setbacks) of paying for placement on certain websites.

How Social Media Activity Increases SEO

A frequent question I often receive surrounds how social media affects SEO. This is hard to answer since social media performance *indirectly* benefits SEO. While not a Google ranking factor, an article in the *Search Engine Journal** summarizes how social media can improve SEO:

---

* Kristopher Jones, "Making Social Media & SEO Work Together," *Search Engine Journal*, November 13, 2024, https://www.searchenginejournal.com/social-media-seo/196185/#close.

- Posting online content on social media boosts the content's performance.

- More people seeing your content increases the chance more will link to it.

- Your social profiles can rank in online searches for branded search terms.

- Good social profiles build trust, harkening back to E-E-A-T.

What helps the most from an SEO standpoint are social posts that are shared a lot, because this sends signals to the search engines. Therefore, not only do we want to post content that is entertaining and helpful, we want to post shareable content. So, consider if someone in your audience would actually share something before you post it.

Paywalls

Many media organizations require paid subscriptions for online access to their content (aka paywalls). You cannot expect to access all news for free simply because you have access to the World Wide Web! Yet some of my clients are reluctant to pitch websites with paywalls. I understand why they may want to reserve their resources for coverage that people can access all the way through, but here is why that's the wrong approach.

The main complaint about earning paywall coverage is that it shouldn't be shared on social media since the story wouldn't be available for everyone to access. But you can recap the story while sharing it in your own social media post. Also, the headline, and possibly the first few sentences of the story, are typically visible before hitting paywalls.

That said, research suggests that articles behind paywalls don't contribute much to SEO, as search engines may not index the full content. However, the type of coverage you'd gain from paywalled media tends to come from high-quality, authoritative outlets—exactly the kind of sources that boost credibility and influence. Even if your coverage comes from a local business journal rather than a national outlet, overlooking paywalled media entirely is a missed opportunity.

Display and PPC Advertising

Let's not forget about the type of online advertising that doesn't behave like an article or blog post in the search engines. Most types of online advertising fit within the following categories:

- Display Ads: The advertiser purchases from a third-party website to visually showcase a brand/product with a CTA that leads to the advertiser's website.

- Google and/or Bing Ads: The advertiser purchases from Google/Bing to appear above the organic results for a keyword or their brand name, but it will be marked as "sponsored" above the result.

One of the ways advertisers can pay for these ads is through pay-per-click (PPC), which means a fee is paid with each click the ad receives. This sounds great, but you want to make sure the clicks you're paying for amount to sales and aren't just empty clicks.

While I'm not aligning this type of online advertising with the PR and organic SEO mentality, it may still fit within your marketing strategy. In fact, online advertising might be the most important marketing piece for a business that sells online. These ads offer valuable tracking benefits that shed light on audience metrics and conversion.

Search Results Within AI Tools

This chapter, along with my scope of knowledge, focuses on SEO within standard search engines like Bing and Google. However, the usurping of AI will force us to examine everything we know about SEO.

Not only is AI already making its way into traditional search results,

ChatGPT has surfaced as one of the top three ways Gen Zs search for information.* This makes sense when you learn that Gen Z's are the only generation to use social platforms over search engines† for shopping-related research.

"Gen Z clearly likes customized results. With over a fifth of 12 - 15 year-olds saying they mainly use social media to find things to buy, it's likely Gen Alpha will have similar search preferences as they age. Brands should future-proof their strategies to include AI," states the GWI study.

While we don't really know how this will affect traditional SEO, I'm future-proofing by first learning how to use AI in my everyday job as a writer and marketer. Then, I will be ready to weather any storm brought by AI. Embark upon this journey with me in the next chapter.

---

* GWI, "The Global Media Landscape."

† "As Seen on Social Media," GWI, accessed March 4, 2025 at https://www.gwi.com/connecting-the -dots/seen-on-social.

CHAPTER THIRTEEN

ENHANCING PR WITH ARTIFICIAL INTELLIGENCE

M any people told me to use Artificial Intelligence (AI) before I was ready. While I'd heard about the wonders of AI, the magical day that it would change my life had not arrived. But once I started experimenting with Chat Generative Pretrained Transformer (ChatGPT), I became so hooked that I started calling it "my boyfriend."

Tools like ChatGPT by OpenAI and Gemini (formerly Bard) by Google are specifically the large language model (LLM) type of AI, meaning they can process and generate data in sequence, resulting in high-quality text. Of course, there are many other AI tools, but my journey started with ChatGPT, and I haven't strayed much from its magnetic grip. While this chapter will close with some limited insight into other tools, I've mostly focused on my experience with ChatGPT.

But before getting into all of that, let's first address how to approach AI. Some are terrified it will replace their jobs, some won't touch it, while others use it indiscriminately. All of these approaches are wrong. Instead of viewing AI with fear, avoidance or indulgence, we can embrace it with an air of experimentation and fun—as long as we apply diligent oversight.

Remembering that AI is not going away, let's harness its powers through the right mindset.

EMBRACE YOUR INNER JOKESTER

One of the intriguing things about ChatGPT is that it can write in the voices of well-known figures, from President Obama, to Ernest Hemingway, to Bart Simpson. So, I started playing around by asking ChatGPT to tell me what Alexis, from the well-loved comedy Schitt's Creek, thinks about a variety of PR topics. She is a PR "professional" on the show after all. :)

When asking ChatGPT to answer questions in Alexis' voice—ranging from what working in PR is like to hiring a PR firm—I received hilarious responses to use in my company's marketing. Not only did I ask ChatGPT to convert some of these responses into social posts, I'm also experimenting with highlighting a version of Alexis in social as a character that's gone on past the life of the show, still living and working in PR.

Approaching AI in this playful way enabled me to look forward to using ChatGPT rather than feeling exasperated. Having fun on the platform may have been instrumental in my transition into using it for more serious work.

MANAGE WITH ANNOYING EDITS

As I moved on to using ChatGPT for more important pieces, such as blog posts and press releases, I recognized the value of boldly asking for revisions. When editing work from human writers, I must walk a fine line between asking for necessary changes and letting things go — so I get what I need while not being too overbearing. Not so with ChatGPT!

I can be as pushy, direct or even downright mean to ChatGPT as I want. In response, ChatGPT can handle revisions ranging from the small, such as adding hashtags and removing jargon, to the large, such as augmenting character voice and adding conceptual depth.

Within the broader picture, it's been eye-opening to see how being direct with ChatGPT has made me uncomfortable. But this exercise has helped me practice clear communication with humans as well.

FLOURISH THROUGH FREE EXPERIMENTATION

Most big things I do begin with an air of experimentation, otherwise my high expectations and perfectionistic tendencies would keep me in limbo. My foray into using AI must replicate this experiential approach as well.

While a few light-hearted social posts featuring Alexis are okay, if I'm being honest, I am worried about over-identifying with a frivolous fictional character. But instead of viewing my ChatGPT gab sessions with her as a waste of time, they may be the catalyst to a new chapter in my life.

AI experimentation has led me to develop the main character, inspired by Alexis, in my first novel. While you may not be using ChatGPT to write your next novel, you can still experiment with AI. We, along with the creators of these tools, have no idea where they might take us, so let's embrace the experiment. While your experimentations may bring a completely different experience, here's what I've discovered through mine.

WHEN TO USE CHATGPT

It's important to remember that ChatGPT is a language processing tool, meaning it works with language to create more of the same. In the marketing arena, this means content. Frustration can build when using ChatGPT for the wrong things.

When I first started using ChatGPT, it had not yet been integrated with DALL-E, which is OpenAI's design tool that can create images and art. So, I was understandably having a hard time creating art in ChatGPT before I realized it wasn't meant for this purpose.

DALL-E has since been added to the interface, but ChatGPT is still unable to create videos. Nor can ChatGPT help you with organization and media list building, which can be confusing because I have read elsewhere that it can. I'm sure there are so many ways to use ChatGPT for PR that I don't even know about, but I have found it to be helpful in the following areas.

Social Media Posts

ChatGPT almost does too well with social media posts, sometimes causing me to wonder if its output was directly lifted from somewhere else. When I asked it to write an April Fool's Day post for my PR agency, it came back with something so good that I searched social media to ensure it hadn't provided the same post to all the PR agencies that had asked for something similar.

While I couldn't find the same post, a few agencies used a similar sentence/post structure. So, I concluded that ChatGPT either picked up this formula from the multiple people already using it online, or spit out this very formula to all that asked for a similar post, but just changed the examples. Either way, it's pretty brilliant.

ChatGPT seems to incorporate humor into its social media posts well. While its more business-oriented posts tend to be a little too professional and vague, without much tone nor insight. But by redirecting at least once, I can typically get something that is passable.

Short Blog Posts and Articles

I never accept ChatGPT's first blog or article draft. I may not like the flow, or something sounds off or just plain wrong. Since Chat-GPT can incorporate misunderstandings into its pieces, I ask it questions while reading its outputs, specifically directing it to answer my questions within its revisions to the piece. This can clear up misunderstandings, bring ownership to the piece and create stronger, and *longer*, pieces.

However, ChatGPT falls short, literally, when it comes to content length. I've never been able to get a piece written by the free version up to 1,000 words, even when I tell it exactly where and how more insight could be added. The first try, in the free version, typically comes back with around 600 words, and after three or so redirections it can sometimes generate around 800 usable words.

The paid version of ChatGPT doesn't seem to be much better at meeting word count. It recently took the paid version about three tries to meet 1,000 words—even though the topic was "how to use Chat-GPT for gaining media coverage"—something it surely should have known about. I was able to increase the word count by asking for more clarification surrounding its overinflated statements about its own PR capabilities.

Press Releases

ChatGPT seems to do well with press releases, as long as you provide it with a detailed outline. This is surprising because press release writing can be quite nuanced, even for experienced human writers.

On the surface, it might seem that press release writing shouldn't be all that hard. But the clean, simple language that press releases require can be difficult for humans to grasp. Moreover, understanding where to place the news hooks and location bits can be challenging.

But I suppose it makes sense that a robot would be adept at creating simple language. And a detailed outline can offer direction about where the news and location bits should be placed in the press release.

Media Pitches

When attempting to use ChatGPT to draft media pitches, I simply give up. While it can usually get the storyline down, it cannot grasp who the audience is (the media!), nor place the closing "asks" at the end of the pitch. I suppose you could augment the audience yourself and add what you're asking for (an interview, run a bylined article, etc.).

The fact that ChatGPT really cannot understand the media relations part of PR points to how specialized PR really is. It can write esoterically about many things, only to falter when getting down to the nuts and bolts of PR.

Edits and Tone Augmentations

ChatGPT seems to be great with cleaning up grammar and sentence structure. It can even handle deeper augmentations around tone. For example, I'll ask it to make something more approachable if it's trying too hard with a professional tone. ChatGPT can also handle writing for unique audiences, although not always perfectly, but with a couple of redirections it eventually comes around.

Character and Persona Development

I'm absolutely blown away by what ChatGPT can do in this area. As I mentioned earlier, I started my foray into ChatGPT by experimenting with the voice of Alexis from Schitt's Creek. At times, it didn't quite understand my direction on audience or purpose, but Alexis' tone was always spot on. Every time I asked for changes, ChatGPT matched my direction and provided completely unique copy, still in her hilarious voice.

All of this character building led me to realize that personas (fictional customer profiles) could be built in ChatGPT to help profile target audiences. Before working on each persona's voice, you've got to understand that audience better. ChatGPT can help with this by asking probing questions about your personas, which provides a jumping off point for persona development through back-and-forth conversations.

Ideation

I'm sure that you can grab a bunch of ideas from ChatGPT. However, I don't use it for that because I tend to have enough ideas within my own crowded brain. But you may be able to brainstorm with ChatGPT to generate ideas around campaigns, events, giveaways, media drops and more. Or going through an ideation exercise with ChatGPT may help you hone existing ideas.

Tedious Tasks

The tedious minutia of our days can be daunting. Sometimes we just cannot handle finishing up a piece of work, whether that's inserting hashtags and emojis into a social media post, or including attention-grabbing subheads into a blog post. In this way, ChatGPT can serve as your assistant, doing all the things that make you go "ugh."

HOW TO USE CHATGPT SUCCESSFULLY

Now that we've covered what types of PR projects you can use Chat-GPT for, it's time to learn how to leverage it to the best of its capabilities.

Practice Ways of Prompting

Success on ChatGPT begins with prompting, which is what you ask in the message bar. I've found two ways of prompting within Chat-GPT that work.

1. Asking for deliverables through multiple prompts within the same conversation. You can have a conversation with it by providing steps one at-a-time, or you can warm it up with a little bit of direction at first and then prompt further.

2. Pasting direction in the form of an outline in the message bar. Outlines are great for longer pieces and can bring results that are more of your own creation, rather than ChatGPT's sometimes regurgitated internet content.

Start and Save New Conversations

ChatGPT will remember tone and instructions for each individual conversation you have with it. Popping back into old conversations to get new tasks completed is useful for similar tasks or tones. Since your previous direction was saved, you won't have to provide as much new direction. You can stay organized by re-wording the way Chat-GPT automatically labels conversations by using your own naming/titling system.

Show it Final Versions

While I've advised you to continue prompting until you get what you want, after a while you may want to copy outputs into a word processing tool to refine them yourself. I'm more comfortable drafting in Google Docs rather than the small messaging bar provided by Chat-GPT. But after I am finished, I will paste my final version into Chat-GPT's messaging bar so it can see what I came up with. Taking extra steps like these can help "train" AI.

Check for Plagiarism

ChatGPT pulls internet content from multiple reference points, so its answers should be mixed up enough to be somewhat unique, rather than regurgitated internet content. And the more you continue offering it direction and rewriting its answers, the more unique you'll make the content. Regardless, all AI-generated content should be checked for plagiarism with a tool like Grammarly or Copyscape.

PAYING FOR CHATGPT

Perhaps all the hype surrounding the paid version of ChatGPT caused my initial disappointment after signing up for it. First, the platform's interface looks almost identical to the free version. This threw me off because I need a better way to organize everything in ChatGPT. For example, I should be able to assign various voices to different clients, or projects, then organize everything within dedicated folders instead of conversations.

But, when I asked ChatGPT how to organize everything within the paid platform, it told me to copy and paste what I needed into a different platform. That's too clunky. And while we can connect ChatGPT with an outside organizational tool, that's yet another platform to manage.

Upon realizing this, I asked ChatGPT to tell me why I should pay for it.

"The upgrade gives you access to the most recent model, which typically offers improved performance, better understanding and **MORE ACCURATE RESPONSES**," ChatGPT responded.

Wait a second. More accurate responses? So, are they providing false answers to the freeloaders?

"Both versions strive for accuracy, but the upgraded version may incorporate newer data, refined algorithms and additional capabilities that can enhance the user experience," ChatGPT responded to my concern.

Well, that sounds a little fishy. While we need to fact check ChatGPT outputs, I just hope that both versions are as accurate as the tech allows for ethics' sake.

More Lengthy Problems

Perhaps it's these extra capabilities from ChatGPT's paid version that cause it to show off with tediously long answers. Sometimes long answers can be useful, but I don't need a listicle for every simple question. Luckily, it seems to understand when I direct it to answer briefly. Also, I use the stop button, near the conversation bar, when ChatGPT seems to be overdoing it.

Possibly more annoying is that the paid version has a hard time being verbose when I need it to be. While it provides long answers to simple questions, even the paid version struggles to hit 1,000 words for a blog post. But, with prodding, I can eventually get the word count to creep up, whereas the free version was never able to hit 1,000 words, no matter what I tried.

New GPT Possibilities

The only thing that currently looks different on the paid version is the "Explore GPTs" section, which brings you to a holding place for all kinds of GPTs. This is where I found the Astrology Birth Chart GPT, which I've been using to create entertaining horoscopes for PR people (sign up to receive yours through my newsletter at veracityagency.com/newsletter-sign-up/).

Moreover, an enticing "Create" button in the "Explore GPTs" area beckons. Apparently, the paid version of ChatGPT can be used to create custom GPTs. Possibly this is where the hype is. I might be able to eliminate all my ChatGPT annoyances by creating my own GPT.

***

After reading my complaints, you may wonder why I call ChatGPT my boyfriend. Let me remind you that not every relationship is perfect. But when something is worth fighting for, we must work hard to make it better. Shortcomings aside, ChatGPT has been an indelible partner and I can't wait to see where this relationship goes next.

ADDITIONAL AI TOOLS

Although I loathe to play the field, I would be remiss not to tell you about other AI tools. Keep in mind that my reviews are *not* coming from a technical expert's point-of-view, so you may have an easier time with these tools. Moreover, these tools will likely progress as AI technology improves, while new tools will undoubtedly be invented each day.

Art and Graphic Design AI Tools

Developed by OpenAI, DALL-E creates images and art from natural language descriptions. In my experience, DALL-E struggled to understand simple directions, and my attempts to make minor design tweaks often resulted in entirely new, unattractive designs that disregarded my original intent. But since DALL-E has been infused into ChatGPT's interface, it's having an easier time incorporating my verbal direction. Imagine that! ChatGPT is a language processing tool after all.

Of course, other design tools exist beyond the OpenAI realm. Midjourney has been praised for its artistic style and high-quality images. Adobe's Firefly is being touted for enhanced workflows and integration into Adobe products. While Canva's Magic Studio has been louted as the best option for beginners — enhancing existing designs rather than generating new images from scratch.

Quite frankly, we **should be cautious about using AI to create images and graphics.** Anything generated by AI in this realm generally cannot be copyrighted, which means that you don't have ownership. Moreover, many graphic designers and artists are witnessing how AI is disrupting their industry. From an ethical standpoint, it's more responsible to create your own designs and use AI to enhance those designs.

Video Creation and Editing AI Tools

Pictory is an AI-powered video creation tool that automatically generates videos from text. From my experience, the images it uses are often clichéd or don't align with my vision. Additionally, I encountered performance issues, with the application stalling and crashing during editing. This led me to conclude that Pictory might only be suitable for very simple videos, such as straightforward product showcases.

Since Pictory was not a good solution, I went back to my non-AI video creation standby, VEED, which didn't crash and stall like Pictory had been doing five minutes before. After quickly getting the hang of it,

VEED has been a delight to use. It also has an AI component that I have yet to try, but I don't see how it could be bad with the original product being so good.

Another text-to-video tool to be aware of is Sora, by OpenAI. At the time of this writing (April 2025), Sora has only been released to Chat-GPT subscribers in the U.S. and is expecting a worldwide release later in 2025.

Customer Insights and Market Research AI Tools

When attempting to gain more information about your audiences, here are two options I've heard about. Brandwatch uses AI for social listening and sentiment analysis and Helixa helps find niche trends through audience intelligence. There are most likely a whole host of additional tools in this arena.

Content Marketing AI Tools

Although it's hard to believe, more LLMs exist besides ChatGPT. Jasper, Writesonic, Microsoft's Copilot and Google's Gemini and NotebookLM are either LLMs themselves or they utilize a combination of LLMs. All of these can be used for content marketing, however NotebookLM is particularly interesting because it was built for research and summarization rather than content generation, although it can turn audio transcripts from podcast episodes or video calls into content.

BETTER WITH AI

AI isn't here to replace creativity—it's here to enhance it. Just as true professionals put their own touch on their work, they don't take AI-generated content at face value. They refine and reshape it, using their expertise to turn something good into something better. For me, AI has become more than just a tool. It's a creative partner that challenges me to think critically and refine my work.

Whether you're experimenting with AI for the first time or honing how you use it, remember that the real power isn't in the technology itself. It's in the professionals who push it further, shape it into something stronger and use it strategically to amplify their expertise. The future of PR, writing and creativity won't be dictated by AI, but by those who make AI work for them.

CHAPTER FOURTEEN

WISE APPROACHES TO CRISES AND RESEARCH

If your organization has only executed a fraction of what's been covered, you're already preparing to mitigate a potential crisis. When organizations are backed by positive media stories and feel-good owned content, they may experience softer landings during hard times. But that's not to say that you don't need to plan for the variety of crises that could befall your organization.

In fact, I suggest embarking upon crisis preparation in a very meticulous way by first outlining each issue that could occur—such as a fire, act of violence, cybersecurity breach, harassment or discrimination lawsuit—then setting aside time to address one scenario each month or every other month. When the allotted time to work on your pre-selected crisis topic rolls around, here is what you'll do:

STAKEHOLDER CONVERSATIONS

Gather stakeholders to discuss the scenario you've been scheduled to address. Here are a few questions to ask them:

- What will be done **during** the crisis to swiftly end it and mitigate damage to staff, customers, products, property, etc.?

- What will be done **after** the crisis to remedy the damage?

- And most importantly, what is being done **now** to prevent the crisis?

Moreover, you'll want to discuss the various iterations of how the crisis could unfold, which may change the answers to the three questions above.

While talking it through, try to understand who would be responsible for completing specific actions during a crisis, such as calling the police, gathering materials, etc. You may not need these details in the external communications plan, but they could help your internal communications plan, and it's better to err on the side of having too much information, rather than too little.

Creating "Response Trees"

Your stakeholder conversations will eventually lead to who will be responsible for specific communications actions—such as releasing the media and staff statements, answering internal questions or serving as a media spokesperson. From this, you'll be able to create what I call a "response tree," which outlines who addresses each part of the communication plan.

The designated person for each action may change depending on the crisis. Moreover, you'll want to assign back-ups for each person listed in case the first designated person is unavailable.

Response trees can branch out into response rules—such as only responding to media via email, no matter how the question comes in, or responding within a set amount of time depending on which audience the question is coming from (staff, partners, media or customers).

Drafting Sample Statements

After digging into such details, hopefully you'll have enough information to create the following:

- Sample all-staff communications, using blanks to fill in where needed, with the distribution schedule and delivery method outlined.

- Sample customer/member/partner communications, using blanks to fill in where needed, with the distribution schedule and delivery method outlined.

- Sample media statements, using blanks to fill in where needed, with the distribution rules outlined. For example, the statement will only be used to respond to media inquiries and won't be proactively released.

There may be specific scenarios for each crisis that require slight tweaks within your statement. For example, a bank robbery isn't just a robbery. Did they target the outside ATMs only? Or did they walk into the location and demand cash from the tellers? Customize the statement for each scenario, audience and format.

We can go deeper from there. Did anyone get injured? If so, what was the outcome? Are they OK, or was there a death? You'll literally want to create sample statements for each outcome. It may seem overkill, but you'll start with one general statement and then tweak it slightly for each situation.

I don't feel the need to create a press release in a crisis. Sometimes less is best. Statements contain enough information, since the media can quote your organization from the statement.

If creating talking points from your statement makes you and your stakeholders feel better, then you should take this extra step. Perhaps also practice the talking points with your spokespeople. But those extra steps may not be necessary. However, **creating draft statements is mandatory.**

Obtaining Approvals

Include a note at the top of your draft statements indicating that you will not release the statement without revisiting it either during the crisis or later down the road with the team. You may have to continuously verbalize this point. Then, put a reminder on your calendar to revisit your proactive crisis plans on a yearly basis to keep them fresh, since it could be years before an actual crisis occurs (if ever).

You may not need everyone to review the entire plan every year, but glance at it yourself to determine if everything's on point. Perhaps you could have the team revisit the plan every other year. However, new team members, stakeholders and spokespeople will need to review the portion of the plan that applies to them—opening it up for changes all over again.

Even though crisis documents can change, you still need to get approval on what you currently have. Because whether the crisis happens tomorrow or a year from now, and your CEO or executive director is on an African safari, at least you'll have something they're OK with.

When getting approval, pass portions of the plan through the appropriate stakeholders for their opinions and ultimate blessing. Pay special attention to the opinions of the subject matter expert associated with each potential scenario. For instance, the head of technology is instrumental in a cybersecurity crisis plan, while the HR department is required for the harassment and discrimination plan. Of course, it's critical to include the CEO or executive director, and possibly the lawyers, in all preparations.

But again, as you're obtaining initial approvals, you're reiterating that the drafts will be continuously revisited to quell any potential nerves.

PLANNED CRISES

There are some large-scale issues that can fall into the crisis landscape. Those might include legislative changes, ownership transitions, massive layoffs, etc. It goes without saying that positive PR leading up to any of these issues can help boost morale among staff, community members and stakeholders. To illustrate, here's a real-life example of working ahead of a planned crisis that goes much deeper than just building that bank of goodwill.

Upon the launch of Cleaner Air Oregon (CAO) — an initiative to bring the country's most stringent air control restrictions to Oregon — the State Department of Environmental Quality (DEQ) identified a pool of 350 Oregon facilities for review.* Our client's manufacturing facility was on that list.

Going through the review process and then making the necessary changes to bring the operation up to the new standards would take years — giving us plenty of time to prepare for the backlash that was to come. Even though our client would be working toward making these updates, they'd now be in the spotlight, with community members and staff questioning what they had — and had not — done.

However, this 120-year-old business had a long history of good deeds. Not only were they providing hundreds of living-wage jobs to residents, they sent any employee that desired through college and then advanced them through the ranks of the company.

We started telling stories like these in monthly blog posts, each accompanied by three social media posts. We covered health and retirement benefits, union details and the safety measures the company put into place to protect those who were working on the ground, especially when it came to protecting them from the air they were breathing.

---

* "Overview of Cleaner Air Oregon," Oregon Department of Environmental Quality, accessed March 9, 2025 at https://www.oregon.gov/deq/aq/cao/pages/cao-overview.aspx.

Blog posts about their strong company culture set a paper trail for angry Oregonians to examine upon hearing about the companies being called into CAO. We wanted people to know about the good things our client had been doing when they scoped them out online.

Then, we incorporated environmental stories into the mix. While my client had a lot of work to do around emissions, they were ahead of the curve in areas like recycling and protecting the surrounding wetlands. We dug into the details, outlining them all.

Eventually, we made our way towards writing about emissions by detailing the items our client was able to address right away, while noting what would be completed after receiving DEQ's instructions. We began addressing CAO head-on through blogs and social media. We made a habit of creating quarterly blog posts, accompanied by social media posts, updating everyone about where we were in the CAO process, what milestones had been reached, etc.

The process would be invaluable to us during a time of crisis. Our interviews with the company's scientists and engineers enabled us to create informative blog posts about each key area. But our approval process helped even more. Our incorrect assumptions could be fixed and the CEO could rephrase a risky line.

It was important that the CEO was comfortable with all of the copy. If she was out of town when something went wrong, I had approved copy should I need it. We discussed that I could use any line from any of our blog posts during an issue, if she wasn't available.

We of course practiced a variety of talking points for every occasion, but I think the blog posts were the most important piece to our preparations. They got us all on the same page, ensuring that the PR team actually understood the issues, while getting our spokespeople comfortable trying on the messaging. And most importantly, we had approved copy.

I would love to tell you about how these preparations helped us act swiftly and expertly during an incident, such as the heated protest I imagined taking place outside the facility. But this company ended up selling to a foreign investor. The air in Oregon would be cleaner, but those emissions were likely going to be transferred overseas.

Even though our preparations were not used to face any real threats, perhaps they contributed to the company's successful sale. With this anecdote from my experience, I hope you can see the value of proactive crisis planning. Not only does preparation bring power, preparation brings peace-of-mind.

HANDLING A CRISIS

Whether or not you have a crisis plan in place, it's easy to lose focus when faced with a high-pressure situation. That's why committing the following concepts to memory is imperative.

Avoid Saying "No Comment"

Every story has multiple perspectives. Help your executives articulate their organization's side of the story rather than resorting to saying "No Comment." While it may appear to be easier, this line of phrasing comes across as insincere.

Time is Critical

Don't spend too much time deliberating about your responses. If you wait too long, the media may steer the story in the wrong direction. Your response doesn't need to be elaborate. It just needs to be timely, clear, concise and accurate.

Always Be Truthful

Regardless of how serious the situation is, you must hold your people accountable. Act as an investigator to uncover what truly happened and present the organization's explanation as accurately as possible. Distorting the truth will only worsen the crisis.

Consider All Audiences

Don't fall into the trap of only focusing on the media during a crisis. Audiences like customers, employees, shareholders and the board of directors can be more critical than the media. Even though the media reaches these audiences, internal stakeholders could feel slighted if they first receive information from a third party. Consider when you will time the release of information both internally and externally, and whether it will be done simultaneously or in a staggered timeline.

Bring in an Expert

If your crisis is severe, don't hesitate to consult a crisis and/or legal expert. But don't let that process delay you. There's no time to spare during a crisis, so avoid interviewing multiple crisis responders and waiting for them to finish other projects before starting yours.

WHEN TO STEP AWAY

Identifying the right moment to remove yourself from a worrisome situation caused by an untrustworthy client, vendor or team member is essential to preserving your professional integrity and personal well-being.

In a crisis, getting to the root of the problem requires asking tough questions. If you sense that you're receiving evasive or insincere answers, trust your intuition and consider disengaging. You can rely on your instincts, even without hard evidence.

Staying true to your integrity may cause some initial financial setbacks, but it will help you build a solid reputation — likely resulting in greater financial success over the long term.

DAY-TO-DAY ETHICS

This chapter has focused on the serious side of crisis management. But it's rare to be faced with the types of situations you read about in the news. Reality lies within the mundane dealings of our everyday lives, where we're called to remain true to our ethics.

What may seem small on the surface can have big consequences if not approached correctly. By focusing on what we can control, perhaps we can avoid costly mistakes. Take research for example. Let's discuss how to conduct and use research properly.

HOW TO RESEARCH ETHICALLY

I've often mentioned that your own research can be infused into your PR and marketing materials. While the internet undeniably provides access to amazing research, we cannot believe everything online. That's not to say that we shouldn't turn to the internet for research, just that we must use caution.

Quality research will help your audiences and the media take you seriously. More importantly, people who release information to the masses have an ethical duty to present honest and accurate information. This starts with backing the statements you make with facts that have been discovered through research.

Here are the ways you can go about research, along with how to cite that research:

SOMEONE ELSE'S
(THIRD-PARTY) RESEARCH

Most PR and marketing statements can be substantiated through third-party research, rather than the organization commissioning their own research. Plus, a lot of everyday research that will enhance your work can be done quickly online.

My four best practices for using third-party quantitative research (which highlights findings through numbers, statistics, percentages, etc.) are:

1. Ensure the data isn't too old. It's OK if the research was from the previous year and even going back a few years. But I cringe when seeing research that's more than five years old because so much can change.

2. Ensure you have a good source. Review Google's E-E-A-T and YMYL principles to learn more about sources. If the research is from an obscure website, they are likely citing another reference. Try to find the original source because credible research is key to having your messages taken seriously.

3. Review participation numbers. Depending on the claim, you may want to ensure a large enough population was tested or polled. A study with 500 participants pales in comparison to a study with 5,000 participants, unless the participants in the larger study do not fit the claim's demographic.

4. Always cite original sources by linking to the source in documents that will be sent or that will live online. When you cannot include the link, reference who commissioned the study and any other relevant details, such as date and demographic information. You may decide to include this information even when you're able to include a link because it makes the piece stronger.

While researching, you might stumble upon an interesting opinion or unique interpretation from another person. By all means, use it! Just attach the person's name, title and organization to a quote you have used, or reference the person when paraphrasing their words. Provide context when needed.

YOUR OWN, FIRST-PARTY, RESEARCH

Of course, when trying to include very important information in your outreach materials, you may choose to commission your own research. Below are ways organizations may conduct their own (first-party) research, starting with the least to the most complex.

Conduct Your Own Survey

Beyond using surveys (through tools like SurveyMonkey) to understand your audiences, surveys can be used to promote findings that align with your key messages or to build creative campaigns. Surveys could be as serious as discovering attitudes toward women and minorities in your industry, or as light as finding the ideal time for your target market to drink their coffee.

What you choose to do with this information is up to you. Of course, you have more leeway with lighter topics, while you need to put extra thought into more serious issues. Your findings can be used in everything from a PR campaign paired with a colorful infographic, to a presentation deck that aims to generate additional funding, and more.

Data From Your Business

A large organization with numerous data points can use its internal figures to signal trends or report interesting findings. You can use positive sales numbers, staffing figures or client patterns to your advantage and work them into blog posts, media pitches, guest articles and more.

When referencing data coming from inside our clients' organizations, we've typically worked with them for a while, so we trust the information they're providing to us. But if you uncover inaccuracies in the data provided by a client or department, move away from referencing it. If you continue receiving faulty data, you may need to address this issue.

Commissioned Research

Some organizations commission their own research with a scientific laboratory, or other reputable organization, such as a university. This is more common for scientific, technical or safety-related research topics. I learned how to use this type of research during the nine years my firm managed PR for a nutritional supplement.

We had a heck of a time battling the poor reputation of the nutritional supplement industry, which is occasionally under fire for false "claims," none of which my client was responsible for. "Claims" are the statements found in the marketing and/or packaging about a product's particular use or benefit. These types of claims are regulated by the Federal Trade Commission (FTC).*

Thankfully, my client commissioned top-notch research. But even quality research can provide less than stellar findings. We refrained from publicizing marginal research results, no matter how tempting it was to make more out of a vague discovery. Not only is it unethical to do so, my client believed that leaning into a shaky claim could hurt revenue in the long run.

Don't Promote All Research

While you can mostly trust research from reputable colleges or institutions, dig a little deeper through Better Business Bureau or *Google News* searches if you're still unsure. Odd discoveries about your scientist/department may halt any actions you'd planned for using the research.

Or your organization may have hired a great research team, only to realize their findings aren't strong enough to use publicly. This is no fault of the research team, nor those who hired this team, the facts are

---

* More information about FTC oversight can be found in this recap of my podcast interview with Douglas Kalman, PhD, former SVP of Scientific and Regulatory Affairs for the Natural Products Association: veracityagency.com/podcast/ethical-dietary-supplement-marketing/.

the facts. Just don't be tempted to use it because you are adept at putting a "spin" on everything.

On the flip side, you may have some great research, but then the scientist or department comes under fire for a personal matter. Although it may be hard, you may need to discontinue referencing the research done by this scientist/department to maintain credibility and integrity.

WORK WITH THOSE YOU TRUST

Today, when I interview potential clients that make bold claims about their organization and its work, I first look to the research. I don't expect a potential client to know that their research should be included in their public-facing materials, but if they're visibly defensive and rebuff the research topic, I walk away quickly.

To be honest, a mere PR pro like myself doesn't really know what type of scientific/technical research is good. That's why we must rely on our instincts and the ethics of others. If someone can't even have a conversation about their research, it may be your only sign that it's weak or nonexistent.

But I don't mean to paint such a negative picture. Quality research that strengthens a previous claim, or brings a new claim to fruition, can make for wondrously successful campaigns—enhancing everything from packaging design and sales sheets to phone scripts and internet fodder. That's why we must remain thoughtful about research at all costs.

EVERYTHING RELATES TO ETHICS

While crises and research may seem like opposite ends of the spectrum, they mesh together, affecting all the other ways to consider ethics in PR and marketing. Everything from how you release information to the media and prepare for a resulting interview, to the way you leverage artificial intelligence and treat teammates can affect something entirely unrelated down the line.

Practicing honest, ethical work will always lead to better results — even if the balance sheet says otherwise. While leaning into the spin can be tempting for the best of us, it's a slippery slope that can quickly spin out of control and diminish any true progress that's been made. Moreover, working with a clean conscience is worth more than the fleeting gains you may obtain through ill-gotten ways.

CHAPTER FIFTEEN

ASSEMBLING AND MANAGING YOUR TEAM

At some point, you may hand off the PR and marketing responsibilities to someone else, if you haven't already. It was smart of you to pick up this book to understand the scope of what you might want to delegate. Not so that you can micromanage your team, but for the opposite reason. With a keen understanding of its inner workings, you'll feel more confident in the people you trust to manage the work.

Marketing and PR teams can come in many shapes and sizes. You may be working towards one of these team structures or a combination of them all:

- **In-House:** The internal group employed by the organization.

- **Agency/Firm:** The external team hired to handle a portion of the work.

- **Freelancer/Contractor:** An independent worker hired on contract and not a formal employee.

- **You!**

Let's examine each of these in more detail.

IN-HOUSE TEAMS

The in-house team can be the most important team on the roster, especially if you are not using an agency or contractor. But even if you are using an external team, their success relies on the efficiency, reactiveness and insight provided by the in-house team. While there is not one way to set up an in-house marketing and PR team, the following roles are key.

Leader

The leader of the marketing team typically serves as an intermediary between top leadership and the PR/marketing team. These decision makers set strategies that align with the overall goals of the organization. In some cases, the PR/marketing leader may also be the organization's founder, CEO or executive director, which increases the value of the manager role to help put the leader's ideas into action.

Perhaps most importantly, the leader sets the team's culture, building a positive and effective working environment that maximizes opportunities for successful outcomes. In the next chapter, you'll learn more about how to build an ideal work environment, along with general ways of managing teams—and yourself.

Manager

Every team needs some sort of "doer." Ideally, they wouldn't also be saddled with executing the other roles listed below. However, there can be some overlap. Regardless, something needs to be done with the work being created, for example managing approvals, pitching press, collecting collateral, etc.

This person is the glue serving as the go-between among various departments inside the organization, while also handling external vendor relationships through facilitating their day-to-day requests. I especially find that an agency or contractor needs to work directly with this type of role, rather than the leader. Often, we just need materials or answers, so this person is key in moving things forward.

Writer/Editor

While most people in the department should be fluid writers, it's helpful to have someone solely dedicated to writing and editing, considering how much we lean on the written word. Blog and social posts, press releases, white papers, case studies, email newsletters, marketing plans and more!

Be sure to reserve your writer's talents for your team. Don't let them get poached by other departments or clients. Even though I suggest you have a full-time writer, pieces can be outsourced to a contractor if necessary.

Designer

From my estimation, a designer is nice to have on the team, but maybe not a must. A lot depends on the organization and industry. If you're in a visual field, such as interior design or fashion, having a designer may take priority over having a writer.

Regardless of the field, a designer is necessary if you're frequently compiling intricate collateral, such as brochures, newsletters, annual reports, etc. Moreover, they can doctor social posts and photos, which can help save a lot of time if you're posting daily on social media.

Since design is mostly computer-based, it makes me wonder if this role can be combined with the digital strategist's, so long as the digital strategist has a keen eye for graphic design.

Digital Strategist

A digitally inclined person is nice to have on the team for uploading pieces to the blog and social media, managing the website/SEO and additional digital assets, such as apps or podcasts.

Moreover, it's important that someone is available to address the many bugs that can pop up ASAP. While bugs could be handled by your IT department, they may be dealing with more pressing issues like cyber-security and ecommerce. That's why it can be beneficial for your team to have its own digital strategist.

Artificial Intelligence

As you become comfortable using AI, you may think that you can forgo one of these roles, or various components of all of them. As discussed previously, AI is at the stage of enhancing our work, not replacing our work. AI can serve as a stand-in for a role that provides tangible items and more likely can assist an overworked employee with components of their jobs.

Other Roles

You may notice that I don't list dedicated PR or social media roles. However, you may call a role whatever you want. If you're set on having a social media manager, but must forgo the designer and/or digital specialist roles, that's fine. The social media person can handle pieces of those roles.

The writing and management roles can morph together as well. While the writer wouldn't work directly with the media, they'd have their hands in the bulk of the work by equipping the PR person (who's likely the manager) with press materials.

Ultimately, team members will bring their specific roles and individual skills to the larger whole so everyone can work together to achieve your objectives.

AGENCIES/FIRMS

When potential clients inquire about working with Veracity, one of the top things they want to know is if we have experience working in their particular field. While it may be a bonus, having experience in your industry shouldn't be the main reason you hire an agency. Most agencies have experience in a wide range of categories that can benefit you.

It's more important to analyze how the agency works as a team and how their structures align with your team's working style. The biggest battles I've had in leading my decades-long agency involve getting our clients to do what's needed so that we can keep delivering results. We've put the following structures in place to do just that:

- Working within an established plan so everyone knows what to expect.

- Checking on progress within the plan and/or adjusting the plan through recurring meetings at least once a month.

- Creating meeting agendas that serve as to-do lists for all teams, essentially organizing the month's work.

- Reporting regularly, not just about media coverage, but also where we are on other actions.

While I've been emphasizing the importance of responsiveness, I realize it's impossible for a leader to respond to every day-to-day need. That's why it's best if a highly organized manager on the internal team can help field agency requests and provide information.

Agency Red Flags

Of course, not every relationship succeeds. Here are several red flags that signal you need to increase your level of engagement or find a new agency partner:

- You don't know what your agency is doing. Your agency

should have a plan that directs their ongoing efforts and they should report results regularly.

- There's no pattern or routine to their work. If your agency's work is scattershot or unpredictable, it could be a sign they're operating without a plan.

- You're coming up with all the new ideas. While I said that active and engaged clients are good, the agency should lead most initiatives.

- You don't see results. If your PR firm isn't delivering results, that's a clear red flag. However, you'll only be able to determine this by establishing critical benchmarks early in your engagement. Otherwise, it will be hard to understand if your efforts are moving the needle.

When in-house teams outsource work, they should be mindful of what will be required. Be honest about how much time you're willing to give an agency. It might be more cost-effective to hire someone in-house to manage the PR/marketing under your guidance. Or consider a part-time contractor that can devote project management time to your organization.

You'll know you're ready for an agency when you have a working internal team structure and some sort of plan that you're consistently executing. After you've gotten into your groove, you'll determine if you can accept another team, another big thing, to manage.

CONTRACTORS/FREELANCERS

Contractors, aka freelancers, are typically self-employed by choice as a means of working with multiple clients. They gain freedom and independence in trade for doing their own paperwork and self-governing their responsibilities.

Contractors must file a W-9 form with the IRS and are responsible for withholding their own taxes. Whereas employers are responsible for withholding taxes on behalf of their employees by filing W-2s. Along with the responsibility of withholding taxes for a W-2 worker comes extra fees and regulations for employers, not to mention the cost of healthcare and other miscellanea.

Contractors can be a fabulous way for organizations to manage their resources. While they'll most likely bring unique insight and experience, a potential downside can be hiring an individual who was laid off or terminated and has turned to independent contracting before they are ready.

Vetting Contractors

To be assured that a potential contractor is self-sufficient before hiring them, here are the questions to consider:

Have They Been Professionally Trained?

Review their work history to determine if they've been professionally trained in the areas you need help with. I typically want to work with contractors that have been trained by someone else and aren't self-taught. I enjoy working with contractors who previously worked for large, respectable PR agencies because I often learn new ways of doing things. And I don't want to risk working with someone who thinks they know what they're doing, but really doesn't.

Why Are They Contracting?

Understanding why someone has moved into contracting can help you select among a pool of candidates. Many turn to contracting as a stop-gap in between jobs. This could be fine, but it's helpful to know your relationship might be temporary. Some people fall into contracting and end up being so good that they stick with it for the rest of their careers. You may want to find those contractors who've been at it for a while.

How Long Have They Been Independent?

I'm more comfortable with contractors that have been successfully independent for at least a few years. This doesn't necessarily mean they're exceptional at their trade, it just means that I can count on them. Sometimes work that is consistent and reliable is more valuable than flash. While those who've been contracting for a while may have higher rates, peace-of-mind may be worth it.

Do They Have the Necessary Tools?

You may have the software or equipment necessary for them to fulfill their tasks, but if they already have these items, it shows how serious they are. For example, graphic designers and videographers may need specific equipment and software. If they have their own, that's one less cost you would otherwise have to incur.

Do They Have Good Work Samples?

People within a creative field, such as writing and design, should have a portfolio of previous work that is accessible online or they should be able to send you samples. Since writing is a big part of PR, I always ask to review writing samples. Sometimes, I can even weed out potential contractors based on how they put a sentence together in an email exchange. If there is one grammatical error, they are out of the running.

Can You Speak With Past Clients?

You may want to call a potential contractor's references. Ask to connect with current or past clients to see if they liked working with this contractor. You might not even reach out to the references, but simply asking for them provides another means to weed out anyone who can't produce any. However, if the contractor has testimonials from past clients on their website, that will probably suffice.

Finding Contractors

There are many ways to find contractors. My preference is to vet contractors through quality referrals or online research. It may seem time-consuming, but you'll save time in the end because a high-quality, hassle-free contractor is more likely to surface this way.

Ask Your Peers

The best way to find a contractor is to ask industry peers who they use. While you could ask by posting a query on social media, connecting directly with your network may yield better results.

Post on Job Boards

If your connections don't turn anything up, you could post queries on job boards that your potential contractor may be looking at, such as the Public Relations Society of America (PRSA) or the American Marketing Association (AMA). There may be a fee to post, but it could be a small price to pay if it connects you with someone you can rely on.

Use an Online Resource

Online resources, such as Fiverr and Upwork, can match you with contractors all over the world. You can set requirements to weed out the intimidating number of options. Provide specific instructions for applying to further weed out candidates, then continue vetting only the contractors that have followed your application instructions by:

1. Reviewing work samples they've uploaded to the platform.

2. Examining past client reviews that have been added to the platform. Consider contractors with longevity on the platform.

3. Speaking with potential contractors. I always want to get them on the phone/video to determine whether they are a real person who can carry on a conversation.

If you end up selecting a contractor through the platform, I suggest using the platform's contract and paying the contractor through the platform. Some people go directly to the contractor to avoid the platform fees. This is not only unethical, but unwise. Paying through the platform will display how much you've paid out to contractors publicly. Good contractors will examine you just as much as you're examining them. They'll be comforted to know you've paid other contractors before they waste time submitting a proposal to a tire-kicker.

In fact, I found a fabulous contractor on Upwork who ended up essentially working for me part-time (as a W-9 worker by her choice, even though I tried to hire her full-time) for almost five years. Working with her was pivotal in my evolution from being a contractor myself, who was used to handling all client work alone, to becoming a full-fledged PR agency, and learning how to delegate and trust that the work would be completed—often better than I could do it myself.

Managing Contractors

After finding a suitable contractor, I make sure to set clear deliverables. For example, a writer may be tasked with delivering four articles to our firm each month, while a designer may be required to deliver three graphics per week. Not only do clear deliverables result in clear expectations, they ensure that the contractor will be used. Otherwise, I'm often tempted to hoard the work, especially if I'm billed on an hourly basis. But keeping all the work for my team is inefficient and becomes impossible with growth.

If you are setting up a new team, or PR/marketing plan, you might not know what deliverables to ask for. But it's still helpful to have a solid contractor waiting in the wings. You could practice handing things off to them, even if you could do the work yourself. A way of working could fall into place while you're practicing delegating.

Practice Delegating With Contractors

Around the time I was working with the contractor I found on Upwork, I was reading Tim Ferriss' *4-Hour Work Week*,* which was a game

---

* Timothy Ferriss, *The 4-Hour Workweek: Escape 9-5, Live Anywhere, and Join the New Rich* (Crown Publishers, 2007).

changer. The book is more about harnessing time through outsourcing work and/or working independently, rather than only working four hours per week.

Ferriss suggests that handing things off to others is a practice we need to ease into doing. Even if we *think* we can do it faster and better. He says that employed people, who may not be able to hire a contractor for work, can practice delegating personal duties to a virtual assistant to build up their future delegating chops and provide a more seamless way to live in the present.

I took Ferriss' advice to heart. After building trust with my contractor from Upwork, I started handing her all client-related items, but in a very slow and measured way. I would proofread and weigh-in on everything, adjusting appropriately. We spent a year kicking things back-and-forth until she learned my style and was off and running. Doing that has forever changed the way I work with new hires and structure client work.

If you don't have the time to manage someone this way, but want to start slowly with a contractor, begin by inserting their deliverables into your PR/marketing plan. Contractors can deliver tangible items (such as creating a social media post), while the in-house team can manage what's done with those items (such as posting and managing interactions).

Contractors for Large Organizations

Let's remember that contractors aren't just for new or small organizations. I met a Fortune 500 marketing head who once equated having a good team of contractors to having a solid "bench"—like how a sports team would have a bench of qualified players who can come in at a moment's notice.

But instead of leaving his bench sitting, he kept them in the game with lower priority work. They were engaged and trained, while also alleviating some of the team's pressures. If an instance occurred—such as staff turnover or a crisis that diverted the team's attention—the pinch hitter could come in already warmed up to pick up the slack.

Take the ABC Test

While I have touted contractors as a great option, employers cannot shirk the responsibility that comes with employing dedicated in-house workers. It's not only my opinion that it's unethical to maneuver all workers into W-9 status, many U.S. states have agreed by adopting the "ABC test." This law classifies workers as independent contractors or not.

According to Cornell Law School,* under the "ABC test," the worker must:

- Be free from the employer's control or direction in performing the work.

- Work outside the usual course of the business and off the site of the business.

- Engage in an independent trade, occupation, profession or business.

Of course, the most well-intentioned regulations will protect some, while harming others. This law originated out of California† in 2020 where it has been notoriously strict, causing many in-state contractors to predict the end of their contracting careers. Not only does the law urge organizations to hire employees, a workaround could push

---

* "ABC test," Legal Information Institute, Cornell Law School, accessed March 7, 2025, at https://www.law.cornell.edu/wex/abc_test#:~:text=The%20ABC%20test%20is%20used,of%20determining%20state%20unemployment%20tax.

† "Worker classification and AB 5," State of California Franchise Tax Board, accessed March 7, 2025, at https://www.ftb.ca.gov/file/business/industries/worker-classification-and-ab-5-faq.html#:~:text=AB%205%20requires%20the%20application,Commission%20(IWC)%20wage%20orders.

organizations to hire out-of-state contractors since the law doesn't apply to contractors living or working outside of the state.

Since I don't live in California, and am not a tax expert, I don't know how this is playing out. I only offer this example to demonstrate that classifying workers as independent must be done with care.

PAYING CONTRACTORS AND AGENCIES

Most contractors want to record the time they spend working on your projects and then bill you for the hours. Putting a dollar amount on time may not only be their problem, it could also be yours. Imagining how the dollars will rack up with each minute they spend, I'm sometimes guilty of making the inefficient decision to keep work in-house.

But paying a new contractor an hourly rate is often a fine way to test a potential partnership. However, you must be clear with your contractor about the maximum amount of hours they should spend on a project. Ask them to warn you once they're approaching their time allotment. At that point, you can decide if you'll let them proceed, or if you'll start reorganizing their time.

You may like paying an hourly rate, not to mention it may be the only way your contractor will bill. But a retainer agreement may also be a viable option. Retainer agreements outline a pre-arranged budget, typically paid each month, for services. My agency only works with clients through retainer agreements and we also employ some of our contractors through retainer agreements in the following ways:

1. By set number of tangible items delivered each month.

2. By time spent per month, evolving into specific responsibilities.

An example of a successful retainer agreement is how we've been working with our writing contractor for years. We pay in bulk for a specific number of pieces each month. Our writer can compile some pieces so quickly that paying hourly would be great for me, but bad for them. While some pieces require so much time that we'd regret starting the project if we were paying hourly.

We get around this by setting up a retainer that outlines the following:

1. How many pieces the writer will deliver each month.

2. How much we will pay each month for the pieces.

Not only does a retainer help me forecast my expenses, the contractor gains peace of mind through guaranteed income.

THE ESSENTIALS OF TIME TRACKING

Even though I rarely pay contractors by the hour, nor do I charge my clients on an hourly basis, we use a time tracking tool called Toggl to record where we're spending time. This helps us understand if we're over-delivering, or worse, under-delivering for each client.

Some people will have their favorite clients, dedicating more time to them, while giving less attention to others. This is unethical if both clients are paying the same retainer amount. Additionally, the longer we work with a client, the more efficient we become. If we have leftover time in the month for a particular client, we should be doing something else for them.

While the hours don't have to be perfect down to the very last second, time tracking widens the minutiae of our days into the big picture, all in one place. In fact, I use time tracking to manage myself.

The next chapter outlines how and why I record time spent, not just on clients, but on personal projects as well. With the following pages focusing on self-management strategies, it may seem that I've skipped the essential topic of how to manage full-time workers. Since my agency is small, I may have less experience managing full-time work-ers than you do. Plus, there are other resources available for gaining that knowledge.

And yet, I believe that everything starts with the self. "Do as I do, not as I say," the saying goes. The way in which we treat and manage our-selves affects not just team culture, but also how effective the market-ing will be. Since success begins with us, the next chapter outlines the tools and strategies I use to be the best boss for myself, which extends toward managing others, whether they are full-time, contractors or even clients.

CHAPTER SIXTEEN

MANAGING YOURSELF

There's too much to do in a day. Besides being bombarded by multiple employee questions, you likely have other responsibilities that could include running an entire organization. Everybody works differently and it would be preposterous to tell you how to run your days. However, I've found that if I manage myself well, the management of everybody else falls into place.

Here's what works for me. Take what could work for you, and leave the rest.

GET YOUR PRIORITIES IN ORDER

There are reasons we're in our current jobs or careers. They may be practical or esoteric, but understanding these reasons can help us make decisions about how we spend our days.

I don't like being pulled in many directions, especially if I did not choose some of those directions. The taskmaster in me has a hard time getting pushed off the path. For example, there are many things to do when raising two kids. It's not that I don't want to do things for my kids, but stopping work for a pediatrician's appointment or a sports practice stresses me out! But if I pause to remember why I created my company in the first place—to allow for family-first flexibility—I feel better about these daily hiccups.

I'm also irritated by the many work distractions that divert me from deeper work, whether that's editing something for an employee or answering a question. When this happens, I remember that I maintain this company to build community and help others—whether they're clients, employees or contractors—realize their full potential. This reframing makes the distractions easier.

Getting in this frame-of-mind helps me realign my priorities. Sometimes a small task given to me by someone else expands my perspective, reminding me that my to-do list sometimes misses the bigger picture.

WORK IN THE FLOW

Three main things affect my working style and deeply relate to each other. I am #1: a creative, #2: with attention deficit hyperactivity disorder (ADHD) and #3: in my reproductive years.

Those with ADHD have a hard time working on things they don't want to work on. I assume most creatives are also this way, and there's probably a lot of crossover between being a creative and having ADHD.

In my dream world, I'd only create. But I sometimes catch myself over-focusing on a project that I would normally consider boring. I want to take advantage of these rare times because we all must do tedious things, so I might as well do them when I'm feeling engaged.

For example, scheduling just a few videos can turn into scheduling out the whole quarter. I wasn't necessarily planning on doing this, and maybe I should have been doing something else, but I got a big chunk of the type of work done that I would have dreaded later.

Interestingly, some weeks I'm absorbed in project management tasks, while other weeks I'm a social butterfly or writer extraordinaire.

Biohack Your Time

It wasn't until reading *In The FLO* by Alisa Vitti* that I understood a fluid way of working isn't just related to my ADHD or quirky creative brain. Apparently, this ebb and flow is biological. Vitti writes that people who are menstruating have two rhythms, the circadian and infradian, while those who aren't menstruating only have the circadian rhythm.

- Circadian rhythms are the changes all bodies experience over a 24-hour cycle.

- Infradian rhythms are the changes menstruating bodies experience throughout their monthly cycles.

People who menstruate experience fluctuating hormones, not just in the span of 24 hours, but also throughout their cycles. What we eat, how we exercise, how we relate with others and even the types of tasks we should focus on are affected by our menstrual cycles.

By focusing on what we're naturally attuned to during specific times in our cycles, we can harness our energy to be effective at work. It's not about getting more done—although that could be a side benefit—it's about doing things at the right time.

If you're no longer menstruating, or never did, there are other ways to biohack your time through maximizing your 24-hour clock, which we'll get to momentarily.

---

* Alisa Vitti, *In the FLO: Unlock Your Hormonal Advantage and Revolutionize Your Life* (HarperOne, 2020).

In The Flo uses the 28-day menstrual cycle* to outline the four phases that influence menstruating bodies for roughly 40 years. They are as follows:

Follicular Phase (7 - 10 days)

With estrogen on the rise, now is the time to focus on creativity and initiating big things. Brainstorming, researching, planning, learning, clarifying vision and launching new projects are examples of what to maximize during this phase.

Ovulation Phase (3 - 4 days)

With estrogen at its highest, now is the time to harness your social butterfly because communicating and collaboration are at their strongest. You'll be at your best if you can schedule big presentations, sales meetings, lunches or collaboration sessions during this phase.

Luteal Phase (10 - 14 days)

With progesterone at its highest, now is the time to cross things off the list. Focusing on getting things done, administrative tasks and organizing projects feels really satisfying right now.

Menstrual Phase (3 - 7 days)

With all hormones being at their low point, now is the time to relax and reflect. Feel okay about rescheduling in-person meetings to allow space for recovering and evaluating where you are in a project or overall campaign. Follow your intuition to realign if necessary.

Being armed with this wisdom, I no longer have ideas that don't go anywhere. I schedule the "doing" of the ideas for a better time. I also try to take advantage of my very short growth window (ovulation) by scheduling presentations and sales meetings during this time. It's okay if these high-pressure activities spill a few days out of the growth time,

---

* With each person's cycle length varying, start tracking yours (perhaps only on paper!) to build a customized schedule of your phases.

because the "growing" hormones aren't completely gone, they are simply lessening. And when I reach the rest (menstrual) phase, I try to be mindful of my in-person commitments.

Now I understand why one week I'm in the groove writing and by the next week I'm happily checking miscellaneous details off a list.

The Circadian Rhythm and Our 24-Clock

While learning about my infradian rhythm was empowering, I have always felt aligned with my circadian rhythm. For instance, I would never squander my morning away with brainless tasks because that's when my brain works best. Ideally, mornings are reserved for writing and complex editing, midday is for client and team work and late afternoon is for what I call "dumb stuff," like scheduling an appointment, paying a bill, deleting emails, etc.

These natural timing instincts made sense after reading *When: The Scientific Secrets of Perfect Timing* by Daniel H. Pink.* Beyond deconstructing the science behind our circadian rhythms and the 24-hour clock, Pink points to research suggesting that human moods, along with energy levels and attention spans, change in the same ways throughout the day, no matter your economic status, ethnicity, gender, age, etc.

Pink wrote that for most of us, happiness rises to a peak about two hours after waking, then comes to a dip in the afternoon and then slowly rises again in the early evening. Calling this the "peak, trough, rebound pattern," Pink says it's the key to the secret of timing that, when unlocked, can unveil the best times to do certain things.

For example, Pink tells people not to schedule surgeries during the afternoon. Since an energy drag accompanies lower afternoon moods, take advantage of the morning, when surgeons and staff are fresh, and moods are bright. Similarly, try to pitch new business or hold

---

* Daniel H. Pink, *When: The Scientific Secrets of Perfect Timing* (Riverhead Books, 2018).

important meetings in the morning. Rapt attentions and better moods among your audience may ensure you're remembered favorably. Let your less-informed competitors take the afternoon slot.

And, if you're not spending quality time with others, embarking on a hobby or making a healthy meal in the early evening—when there's a rise in mood and energy—Pink suggests using this time for a second wave of working.

Why follow the typical nine-to-five working day when we're at our worst performance after lunch? Possibly extend that lunch break for some R&R or get a nagging errand done. Return to work around the early evening to ride the lift-off in mood and energy.

Individual Chronotypes

While these moods and energy levels paint a common picture for most, not all of us are made the same way. Everyone has a slightly unique chronotype, which Pink defines as "the personal pattern of circadian rhythms that influence our physiology and psychology." A simple three-question test in his book can determine your chronotype.

There are three general chronotypes: the lark (early to bed, early to rise), the owl (late to bed, late to rise) and falling somewhere in the middle is what Pink calls the "third bird," which makes up about 60 to 80 percent of us. When not ruled by the alarm clock, or kept up by screens, third birds (of which I am one) would naturally wake around 7 a.m. and fall asleep around 11 p.m.

These differing internal schedules mean we're better at certain types of tasks during certain times of the day, depending on the chronotype. Larks and third birds experience the day in this order: peak, trough and rebound stages. But interestingly, owls experience the three stages in the reverse order: recovery, trough, peak.

After discovering our chronotypes, Pink advises: "If you have even modest control over your schedule, try to nudge your most important work which usually requires vigilance and clear thinking into the peak and push your second most important work or tasks that benefit from disinhibition into the rebound. Whatever you do, do not let mundane tasks creep into your peak."

Allowing Others to Peak

It makes sense to harness your team's energy and moods at the time that works best for them—not you. "If you're a boss, understand these… patterns and allow people to protect their peak," Pink advises. Not only will you get better outcomes, your team will love you for it, which is priceless in this job switching culture.

You may feel more comfortable doing this by providing a window, such as 10 a.m. to 2 p.m., when everyone is working at the same time. Team members can get additional work done at the top or the end of those hours, depending on their chronotype. Or you can explore different ways of meeting and reporting, not only to ensure things are getting done, but to keep yourself available to your team as well.

If you can adjust your thinking from valuing time on paper (how long somebody works), to output (results and value), things will improve. Some may work faster than others, which our capitalist society values. But working at one's own pace, possibly slowly, can disinhibit creativity and provide space for the type of detail orientation that prevents mistakes.

If being flexible with time sounds outrageous, possibly the best way to adjust your thinking is to start with yourself. Determine your chronotype and attempt to work in a way that maximizes your style. After doing so, you may be more comfortable letting your team work this way as well.

BATCH WORK EVERYTHING

Another way to manage yourself well is to group similar tasks together and complete them within the same timeframe. Let's call this "batch working." Working with your chronotype and/or in a flow state leads to a more seamless way of batch working.

For example, after my first book, *A Modern Guide to Public Relations*, came out, I released a 60-part video series teaching portions of the book on a weekly basis. It may have appeared that I recorded one video each week. But no, I recorded as many videos as I could get through, ranging between four to eight, every Friday afternoon. I'm not too proud to admit that I stopped for an outfit change in between each video to make it appear like I was recording on different days.

The way this video series began is a great example of my three main qualities—creative, ADHD and reproductive years—in action. After writing this first book, my partner asked me to record "a few videos" about it. Well, I must have been in the outgoing, growth stage of my cycle because what started with a "few videos" turned into much more.

As I started recording that first day, I pulled a classic ADHD hyper-focus by narrowing in to explain each section within the book. The recording equipment was already set up and I was in the flow. So, I took hold of the moment and batch-worked eight videos in one afternoon, which was more efficient than having to get set up all over again eight separate times. If I hadn't let my enthusiasm take over that day, the series would be nonexistent.

Sure, I wasn't always in the mood to record on Friday afternoons, but it had already become my schedule so I trudged through it, sometimes only recording three videos in an afternoon until I finished the series. However, a social media manager with their heart set on posting one video per week just got three weeks of content from my half of an afternoon. Sometimes, in the moment, I'd wonder if I was wasting my time, but years later, when I was still running those videos, I thanked my past enthusiastic self because by then I sure wasn't in the mood to record a video!

Interestingly, once I get going on a task, I want to continue doing that type of task, even if it is mundane. Just getting started is the hardest part of anything, which is probably why batch working is so helpful. And ADHD'ers especially have a hard time switching between projects.

Not only do I try to batch similar types of work together, I try to only work on one client at a time. Since we record the time we spend working on client projects, it's inefficient to stop working on one client to answer a question regarding a different client. Not only would I have to switch my recording time, I'd have to open a different document or get in a different headspace to answer the question. So, working on one client at a time provides me with the discipline required for batch working.

TRACK YOUR OWN TIME

Even if you aren't in the habit of recording your time or working on multiple clients, I recommend using a time tracking tool. You can download Toggl for free and still access the reporting and stopwatch function. In-house teams can approach working on different projects, departments or functions as if they were separate clients—entering each into a time tracking tool.

While Veracity is my agency, and not my client, I still want to know how long we spend on various agency functions. Not only does time tracking prevent the inefficiencies of multi-tasking, it nudges me toward doing things I don't want to do. Sometimes, I give myself a time requirement to work on sales for Veracity. Simply opening the time-tracking tool and selecting sales is the first easy step to working on something I'd rather not do. I can look back at the time spent and feel that I accomplished something by at least racking up some hours on this dreaded, but necessary, business function.

Let's say your team is tasked with supporting multiple departments. Prioritizing how much time should be spent on each, based on current needs or objectives, can help you set time limits or requirements for each department. If one department becomes too needy in comparison to another, past time reports can provide proof for making a change. There's nothing like time tracking to keep yourself accountable and help you understand when you need to adjust.

If time tracking is new to your organization, a major caveat is that employees may feel like they're being monitored. It wouldn't be wise to spring this on employees who've recently adopted hybrid work and crave independence.

Start small (if you think it's worth it) by:

- Encouraging employees to individually practice time-tracking to learn balance and self-management.

- Ensuring employees that you won't review their time reports because you don't have access to their personal accounts.

- Nudging employees who like using it to invite contractors or vendors they're managing to record time spent on their projects.

- Communicating that not all time at work is recorded. Six hours of time recorded in a day doesn't mean a full eight-hour day hasn't been put in. We are not machines. Whether working from the office or home, we need water and restroom breaks, or distractions like answering the door, loading the latest Zoom version, etc. will happen. And often, the best ideas arise while at the proverbial water cooler—long after the timer has stopped.

DELEGATE AS MUCH AS POSSIBLE

You're inevitably adding more to your to-do list by hoarding the so-called hard thing, fast thing or generous thing. Even if you think you can do something faster than somebody else, you can't. Trust me, I've tried. I used to think I was doing people favors by handling most things myself. However, I've come to realize that hoarding some work from junior team members can be selfish.

It's wonderful to provide ample training in the early days of a new hire, but then it's essential to back off once they've got the hang of it. While fully giving up the reins can be a slow process, it's quite liberating.

More than benefiting my mental health, this release of control provides better results. I've realized that my clients are in better hands with my employees than if I were solely running the show. Of course, I still oversee client strategy and advise on media approaches, but I'm busy with other things. My team members actually have the time to provide better client service than I do.

While I still attend client meetings, I try to keep my mouth shut. Letting my employees lead builds their confidence and presentation skills, and positions them favorably. Not only do my team members know more about each client than I do, they're in the trenches with the media, so oftentimes they'll understand the best media strategies as well.

Above all, your team knows more than you think they do.

How to Delegate

While I write about handing over the reins, trusting others with something as important as PR and marketing can be challenging. If you're completely unaware of what's going on, you won't be able to build the type of trust necessary for advancing your organization. That's why I use the following ways to keep everyone, from internal teams to clients, informed so that we can work independently, together.

Planning With Calendars

Planning ahead by maintaining a calendar that outlines when actions will take place keeps everyone on the same page, reminds people to do things and serves as a communication tool so that you don't have to wonder what everyone is doing. Adding a status section to calendar items can further that communication, so all you have to do is check the calendar for an update on specific items. A project management tool may take the place of the calendar and/or status updates.

Recurring Meetings

Setting aside a conscious amount of time for everyone to check-in keeps things rolling, while bringing flexibility. Regular meetings allow you to delete what's not working in your plan and add new opportunities to your plan. I would suggest meeting on a monthly basis at a minimum. Internal teams could maintain bi-monthly, weekly or even daily meetings depending on how active your marketing work is.

Remaining Responsive

If you find yourself wondering why things take a little while, take a look at yourself. In my experience, the people executing the work are constantly waiting for their bosses or clients to deliver items or information to them. While recurring meetings can provide a good reminder, you're holding your team up if you're not responding to their needs as they come in.

However, being responsive is not a competition in who can write the fastest email. We'd rather wait a few days to get a proper reply rather than a cryptic answer sent immediately. Not only do cryptic answers stall us — since we're deciphering your meaning and plotting how we're going to reapproach you for further clarification — we could move forward with wrong information and possibly make mistakes.

KNOW BEFORE YOU GO: PR HANDOFF

After responsibilities have been handed over, remember that PR is nuanced and complex. You might think an idea should amount to reams of media coverage and blame your team if this doesn't happen. While the coverage that they gain may be modest, any progress is better than none. Often fewer, yet targeted, placements can be more valuable than a bunch of random media mentions.

While I did mention that you might examine your response times if your team seems to be moving slowly, it's important to remember that PR is a time-intensive field, and it's easy to underestimate how long each step takes. Patience is essential when you hand over the reins. Give your team the space to work methodically, with their care and attention serving as a testament to their commitment.

It's crucial to listen and understand your team's perspective. Since they are on the frontlines, their insights can provide a better picture of what might succeed or fail. By creating an environment where open dialogue is encouraged, you'll help prevent costly mistakes and enable your team to grow from their experiences. At times, when disagreements arise, explaining your perspective ensures they learn and evolve.

Finally, practice what you preach. Leading by example, particularly when it comes to how you govern yourself, sets the standard for your entire organization. There will be times when stepping back communicates more trust and empowerment than diving in. By focusing on your own goals and actions, your confidence in your team will grow, and they will rise to meet your expectations, ultimately strengthening your overall PR efforts.

CHAPTER SEVENTEEN

PUTTING IT ALL TOGETHER

W̵ith planning being integral to the inner-workings of a team, I will leave you with ways to create your own plan. We use Google Sheets for all client plans, but Excel or another program will work too. Multiple tabs (separate sheets within the same worksheet file) help us capture details or organize by category. But we keep the first tab within our plans simple and high-level to allow for quick visualization of what's coming up. The exercises below are meant to help you create the first tab of your plan.

Follow along with me by reviewing the two sample plans I've provided for fictitious companies at the end of this chapter, along with a template you can make your own. The template can be downloaded at https://www.veracityagency.com/pr-planning-template/.

But, first things first, what's new with you?

"YOURS" ALLEVIATES THE NEED FOR IDEAS

When staring at a blank page, it can be hard to develop ideas. But you don't have to come up with new ideas right now. It's more important to first consider what's going on in your organization or with its top leaders—otherwise known as "Yours." Consider the following:

- What new things are happening now?

- What will be happening a few months from now?

- What will be happening six months to a year from now?

Updates about your organization—such as new products, services or initiatives—are the types of things we're looking for here. Since the news covers what's new, many of these items could be prime opportunities for media outreach, while also serving other marketing efforts. However, at this juncture we don't need to know what we'll do with these items.

If you roughly know the month when something will occur, add it to the Yours section of the planning template. Or, keep items in a separate list to be added to the Yours section when you have more clarity.

"THEIRS" PROVIDES AN OUTSIDE PURVIEW

Now that you've sketched what's going on inside your organization, it's time to look outside your organization. Consider what your audiences are paying attention to. For example, what might they be putting on their own calendars or planning for?

Either within the "Theirs" section of the template, or in a list, answer the following questions:

- What industry events or trade shows are coming up?

- Are there any community happenings your audiences may attend or care about?

Go ahead and add events you already know about, even if you're unsure about your organization's level of involvement. You may not even attend an event, but you can still consider timing marketing efforts around it—such as distributing a press release to coincide with a major industry gathering or posting about an event on social media.

After considering what's already top of mind, you'll want to spend some time researching, like checking dates and cross-referencing lists to ensure you're not missing anything. During this type of research, I'll typically create a messy list, copying and pasting details that I find online into a Google Doc to be assessed and added to the plan later.

"EXTRA" BRINGS VARIETY AND NUANCE

The third section of the plan, titled "Extra," is for holidays, national observances and quirky dates that add playfulness or variety. We use National Day Calendar to find this information, adding almost everything that relates into the Extra section.

After adding more and more National Day Calendar entries, the Extra section can sometimes become trite. But we don't use most of what's added here as it's primarily meant to provide ideas when we're stuck. For example, our media pitches can lead with some timely dates, while light-hearted themes like National Donut Day help us fill the social content pipeline.

But sometimes we'll come across important themes—such as Breast Cancer Awareness Month or Earth Day—to tie into larger initiatives. This section also reminds us of holidays that we should plan ahead for, such as Valentine's Day for chocolatiers or Memorial Day for campgrounds.

While recurring seasonal themes, such as back-to-school, could be added here, we'll often highlight one seasonal theme per quarter at the top of the plan (near where the months are listed) to set the tone for the quarter. Regardless of where you list seasonal themes, this research will likely bring the theme out from hiding.

"DOING" GUIDES YOUR ACTIONS

It doesn't help to have a bunch of broad entries listed in the plan without an understanding of what you'll *do* with them. That's what the "Doing" section is for, found in between the Theirs and Extra sections. Start adding any action-oriented ideas that your broad entries inspire here. Or turn to the Audiences section of this chapter if you have too many ideas and are having trouble focusing.

The two action-oriented categories we'll focus on in the Doing section are media outreach and owned content. While you can add more categories, let's focus on the basics. Let me explain a little more about each.

Media Outreach Frequency

First of all, media outreach doesn't need to occur every month. Reaching out once a quarter is fine, or perhaps the Yours section will dictate your schedule. You can increase media outreach depending on your "news" or how active your team wants to be. For instance, you could add rows in the earned media section signifying when editorial calendars or bylined articles will be pitched.

Owned Content Frequency

Publishing new website content at least once a month is non-negotiable for maintaining or increasing SEO. While I'm envisioning this content to come in the form of blog posts, it could exist in the form of podcast episodes or videos.

The solid cadence of a monthly blogging schedule can serve as the starting point for other marketing activities, such as media pitches, email newsletter content or social media posts. Moreover, we typically assign three distinct social media posts for every blog post we write.

While content topics can stem from the Theirs and Extra sections, let's not forget AI. After filling out the Theirs and Extra sections of my fictitious plans, I wasn't sure what blog topics to include. So I asked

ChatGPT for ideas, specifying which months needed topics and that they should align with seasonal themes. Even though I didn't define what those seasonal themes might have been, ChatGPT's suggestions aligned so well with the themes I already had in mind that I started questioning my own research process. (But I'll save that for another book—perhaps on how to fully integrate AI in marketing and PR!)

THE INTRICACIES OF TIMING

Right now, our plan lists when actions need to be completed, not when work commences—leaving little time to work ahead. In other words, the actions are currently falling during the months the marketing needs to go out the door or when the media coverage needs to land. Therefore, it's also helpful to visualize when your team should begin each effort.

Below are a few ways to do this, or you could create your own method, so long as you're mindful of media lead times, approval timeframes and how everything lines up with other activities and priorities.

- **Add additional rows** within the same worksheet tab to signify when work on each action commences. Highlight these rows in a different color to differentiate them from other rows.

- **Create a new tab** within the worksheet that details when specific activities for each action need to occur. With the extra space, you can signify who's in charge of each piece or provide status updates.

- **Block out time** to work on each deliverable, or set internal/personal deadlines, either within your own calendar or a new calendar that can be overlaid on top of your personal calendar and/or the calendar that is shared with other members of your team. This can be done through Google Calendar, Outlook, Teams, etc.

- **Use a project management tool** by moving all actions and deadlines into it. Some tools that work well include Monday or Asana.

ALIGNING WITH AUDIENCES

If you're distracted or discouraged by too many ideas, take a minute to see how everything lines up with your audiences. To narrow your focus and keep the workload manageable, try to **keep the number of audience types you'll target to four or less.**

Fill in the audiences portion at the top of the plan. Glancing at your audiences as you work will help you consider how impactful each entry will be to each audience. After your plan is filled out, use the audience tally at the bottom to see if you're comfortable with the emphasis on one audience over another in the "Doing" section.

As discussed in Chapter One, you can avoid placing too much emphasis on one audience type over another by assigning a prioritizing scale to each audience. The prioritizing scale could guide what you choose to focus on. For example, Audience A could receive 60% of your focus, while Audiences B and C each receive 20%.

Of course, nothing is ever this straightforward, but maybe your prioritizing scale can help you eliminate some broad entries or detailed actions.

Selecting Audiences

The following questions can help you uncover your audiences if you're uncertain. A set of questions is meant to help businesses, while another set is for nonprofit organizations. Remember to be lean and mean with your answers so you're not saddled with more than four audiences, because trying to go beyond four can be overwhelming and inefficient.

Audiences for Businesses

Many types of businesses can begin selecting their audiences by answering the following questions:

- Who are your main customers?

    » Consider the demographics of your top two types of purchasers, including current and potential customers.

- Who is your main referral source?

    » Or who would you like it to be? If you have more than one referral source, list them in order of importance, but limit this to one or two more.

- What trade industry is your organization in?

    » Your trade is the industry that you work within (PR and marketing for me).

If you have more than four audiences, marketing to your trade may be unnecessary and/or you could delete one of the above audiences to stay under four total. You can add additional audiences as your marketing progresses, but let's keep it simple in the early planning stages.

Audiences for Nonprofits

Many types of nonprofit organizations can begin selecting their audiences by answering the following questions:

- Who are your donors?

    » Consider the demographics of your top two types of donors.

- What government source/foundation supports you?

    » Consider the demographics of your top two types of decision makers.

- Who helps you?

  » This is your helper audience, such as volunteers and galvanizers like your board of directors, advisory board or other influencers.

- Who are you helping?

  » This is your beneficiary audience and could be considered a deeper trade that extends beyond the too general nonprofit trade.

In reality, nonprofits may end up with more than four audiences, but hopefully audiences can be combined. For instance, your donor audience may match your helper audience, while providing educational marketing to your beneficiary audience may inform all audiences about your mission and deepen support.

A FRAMEWORK THAT ADAPTS

While the structured approach I have outlined will set your foundation, remember that the insights you've gained here aren't meant to be rigid. Instead, they'll help you create a flexible plan that can be shaped as your actions bring new insights.

Moving forward, trust your instincts, stay curious and be willing to adapt. PR and marketing thrive on creativity, strategic thinking and the ability to anticipate and respond to change. Each campaign you execute, every piece of content you publish and every relationship you nurture will sharpen your expertise and deepen your impact.

MAKING YOUR OWN WAY

You've made it to the end of this book, but in many ways, this is just the beginning. Throughout these chapters, we've explored the intricacies of PR and marketing, dissecting best practices you can use to elevate your brand's presence and engagement. Now, it's time to put this knowledge into action.

You have the tools, but more importantly, you have the ability to take them further. Whether you're improving SEO, developing a content calendar or strengthening your thought leadership presence, know that you have what it takes to not only apply what you've learned but to innovate upon it.

This is your moment to step forward with confidence. Keeping your goals in mind, experiment boldly and refine your approach over time. Those who are successful with their PR and marketing don't just follow best practices—they shape them.

PLAN EXAMPLES AND TEMPLATE

B2B Marketing Plan Example: Human Resources (HR) Software

Trade Audience: Human Resources (HR)

Vertical Audiences: Healthcare, Sustainability

	QUARTER 1			QUARTER 2		
	JANUARY	**FEBRUARY**	**MARCH**	**APRIL**	**MAY**	**JUNE**
YOURS	Sustainability Product Update		New Branch Office Opening		New Advisory Board	
THEIRS		GreenBiz Conference	HIMSS Global Health Conference & Exhibition		Unleash America (HR "Festival")	SHRM25 (HR Conference)
DOING						
Owned Blogs	New Year, New HR Goals: Streamlining Workforce Management	How HR Tech Supports Green Initiatives	Healthcare HR Readiness: Staffing & Compliance	Earth Month: HR Tech for a Sustainable Workforce	Nurse Burnout: How HR Tech Can Help (for National Nurses Month)	Summer Workforce Strategies: Seasonal Hiring & Flexibility
Press Releases		Release Sustainability Product Update at GreenBiz	Release New Office (Trades)		Release New Advisory Board (Trades)	
EXTRA	1/1 New Year's Day National Fun at Work Day (Last Fri. in Jan.)	2/14 Valentine's Day 2/20 National Leadership Day	Women's History Month 3/8 International Women's Day National Employee Appreciation Day (First Fri. in March)	Earth Month Stress Awareness Month National Employee Benefits Day (date varies) 4/7 World Health Day 4/22 Earth Day	National Nurses Month Global Employee Health & Fitness Month Mother's Day (Second Sun. in May) Memorial Day (Last Mon. in May)	Pride Month Leave the Office Early Day (First Mon. in June) 6/19 Juneteenth Take Back the Lunch Break Day (Third Fri. in June)
AUDIENCE*		SUSTAINABILITY X 2	HEALTHCARE	SUSTAINABILITY	HEALTHCARE	

*Actions from the "Doing" section have been tallied. Since every campaign will be augmented for the trade audience (HR), we did not tally HR campaigns. Instead, we tallied the verticals (sustainability and healthcare) to ensure a balanced approach. Sustainability: 4 actions in the Doing section. Healthcare: 4 actions in the Doing section.

B2B Marketing Plan Example: Human Resources (HR) Software

Trade Audience: Human Resources (HR)

Vertical Audiences: Healthcare, Sustainability

	QUARTER 3			QUARTER 4		
	JULY	**AUGUST**	**SEPTEMBER**	**OCTOBER**	**NOVEMBER**	**DECEMBER**
YOURS	New AI Integration with Platform	Testing AI Integration			Holiday Promotion Tied to Charity	Continue Promotion/Giving Tuesday
THEIRS			Advanced Practice Provider Leadership Summit		Thanksgiving	Holidays
DOING						
Owned Bogs	Sustainability Workforce Challenges with AI	Back to Business: Retention & Engagement Before Q4	Workforce Development Month: Upskilling with HR Tech	Year-End Compliance: HR Policy & Labor Law Updates	Healthcare Open Enrollment Season	Looking Ahead to 2026: HR Tech Trends
Press Releases			Release AI Integration at Leadership Summit		Release Beneficiary Charity	Release Amount Raised for Charity
EXTRA	7/4 Independence Day 7/25 Hire a Veteran Day National Intern Day (Last Thurs. in July)	National Wellness Month 8/26 Women's Equality Day	National Clean Up Day (Third Sat. in Sept.) Women's Health & Fitness Day (Last Wed. in Sept.)	10/1 National Green City Day Clean Your Virtual Desktop Day (Third Mon. in Oct.)	National Stress Awareness Day (First Wed. in Nov.) 11/15 National Philanthropy Day 11/15 America Recycles Day Giving Tuesday (Tues. after Thanksgiving)	Holiday Season
AUDIENCE*		SUSTAINABILITY X 2	HEALTHCARE	SUSTAINABILITY	HEALTHCARE	

*Actions from the "Doing" section have been tallied. Since every campaign will be augmented for the trade audience (HR), we did not tally HR campaigns. Instead, we tallied the verticals (sustainability and healthcare) to ensure a balanced approach. Sustainability: 4 actions in the Doing section. Healthcare: 4 actions in the Doing section.

Consumer Marketing Plan Example: Vegan Granola Bar

Trade Audience: Food Merchandisers

Vertical Audiences: Fitness Enthusiasts, Parents

	QUARTER 1			QUARTER 2		
	JANUARY	**FEBRUARY**	**MARCH**	**APRIL**	**MAY**	**JUNE**
YOURS	First-Party Research Results In (wait for Expo West to announce)	Release Valentine's Flavor				
THEIRS	Tastemaker Conference	Valentine's Day	Natural Products Expo West	Influencer Marketing Show	Mother's Day	College & High School Graduation
DOING						
Owned Blogs	Fuel Your New Year Fitness Goals with Plant-Based Power	Ingredients that Boost the Love Hormone (Oxytocin)	Spring into Snack Time: Healthier Grab-and-Go Options for Busy Families	Explain Research Results in a Consumer Friendly Way	5 Easy Ways to Refresh Your Fitness Routine This Spring	Summer Snack Hacks Every Parent Needs
Press Releases		Announce New Flavor with Vitamins D & C (Oxytocin Stimulants)	Release Research Results / Sample New Flavor (at Expo West)			
EXTRA	1/1 New Years Day 1/21 National Granola Bar Day	American Heart Month National Snack Food Month 2/14 Valentine's Day	National Nutrition Month 3/8 International Women's Day 3/12 National Working Mom's Day (date may shift)	Stress Awareness Month 4/1 April Fools Day 4/6 National Student Athlete Day 4/7 World Health Day	Global Employee Health & Fitness Month National Fitness Day (First Sat. in May) Mother's Day (Second Sun. in May) Memorial Day (Last Mon. in May)	Pride Month 6/6 National Higher Education Day 6/19 Juneteenth Father's Day (Third Sun. in June)
AUDIENCE*	FITNESS		FAMILIES		FITNESS	

*Actions from the "Doing" section have been tallied. Since every campaign will be augmented for the trade audience (food), we did not tally food campaigns. Instead, the verticals (fitness and families) have been tallied to ensure a balanced approach. Fitness: 6 actions in the Doing section. Families: 4 actions in the Doing section.

Consumer Marketing Plan Example: Vegan Granola Bar

Trade Audience: Food Merchandisers

Vertical Audiences: Fitness Enthusiasts, Parents

	QUARTER 3			QUARTER 4		
	JULY	AUGUST	SEPTEMBER	OCTOBER	NOVEMBER	DECEMBER
YOURS						
	New Delivery System (gels)			Sponsor Marathon	Holiday Promotion Tied to Charity	Continue Promotion/ Giving Tuesday
THEIRS						
		Vegan Food Bloggers Convention	Back to School	Marathon in Headquarter Location	Thanksgiving	Holidays
DOING						
Owned Bogs	Sweat Smart: Best Plant-Based Snacks for Hot-Weather Workouts	Back-to-School, Back to Healthy Habits	Science of Brain Foods Explained	Protein Fueled Vegan Swaps for Runners	Highlight Beneficiary Charity	Guilt-Free Indulgence for the Festive Season
Press Releases	Announce New Delivery System: Gels for Workouts			Announce Involvement with Marathon	Announce Beneficiary Charity	Announce How Much Raised for Charity
EXTRA						
	National Picnic Month 7/4 Independence Day National Parents' Day (Fourth Sun. in July)	National Wellness Month National Back to School Month 8/26 Women's Equality Day	National Women's Health & Fitness Day (Last Wed. in Sept.) National Family Health & Fitness Day (Last Sat. in Sept.) 9/25 National Daughters Day 9/28 National Sons Day	Self Improvement Month National Walk to School Day (date varies) 10/16 National Sports Day	World Vegan Month 11/1 World Vegan Day National Stress Awareness Day (First Wed. in Nov.) Small Business Saturday (Sat. after Thanksgiving) Giving Tuesday (Tues. after Thanksgiving)	Holiday Season
AUDIENCE*	FITNESS X 2	FAMILIES	FAMILIES	FITNESS X 2		

*Actions from the "Doing" section have been tallied. Since every campaign will be augmented for the trade audience (food), we did not tally food campaigns. Instead, the verticals (fitness and families) have been tallied to ensure a balanced approach. Fitness: 6 actions in the Doing section. Families: 4 actions in the Doing section.

Marketing Plan Template

Trade Audience:

Vertical Audiences:

	QUARTER 1			QUARTER 2		
	JANUARY	FEBRUARY	MARCH	APRIL	MAY	JUNE
YOURS						
THEIRS						
DOING						
Owned Blogs						
Press Releases						
EXTRA						
AUDIENCE*						

*Tally vertical audiences reached in "Doing" section.

Marketing Plan Template

Trade Audience:

Vertical Audiences:

| | QUARTER 3 | | | QUARTER 4 | | |
	JULY	AUGUST	SEPTEMBER	OCTOBER	NOVEMBER	DECEMBER
YOURS						
THEIRS						
DOING						
Owned Bogs						
Press Releases						
EXTRA						
AUDIENCE*						

*Tally vertical audiences reached in "Doing" section.

ACKNOWLEDGEMENTS

Thank you to the ultimate wing woman, Cailyn Tegel. I would never have finished this book without your steadfast dedication to our clients and the emotional support you so freely provide. Debra Flickinger, know that you will always be my editor, retired or not. Your indelible advice, from yesterday and twenty years ago, will continue to ring in my head as my fingers pound the keyboard today and twenty years from now.

Thank you to my parents for your unwavering support. Dad, it's so comforting to know you're always in my corner, the safekeeper of all important things. Mom, your entrepreneurial spirit showed us how to design a life of our own making. Brother, you inspire and motivate everyone around you.

To my Saturday morning group, especially the coffee queens, you're the highlight of my week—extending into months, years, a lifetime of commitment to each other.

And last, but never least, my core crew. Mike, your partnership in everything makes anything possible. Thank you for all you do for our family. Ben, you have grown in so many ways. I already miss making your oatmeal, but I'm excited to see where this next chapter takes you. Audrey, I love watching you come into yourself, standing strong in who you are. You lead in more ways than you know.

ABOUT THE AUTHOR

Amy Rosenberg learned PR in the trenches—working her way up from intern to management at two marketing agencies before starting her own PR firm, Veracity, in 2008. As the firm's president, Amy oversees the blending of digital strategies with classic PR tactics to increase everything from SEO to community engagement for select clients.

Amy's first book, *A Modern Guide to Public Relations*, was released in 2021, with an extensive video series further explaining the concepts. Her podcast, PR Talk, sponsored by the Public Relations Society of America (Oregon), is on pause but available for download—offering over 100 interviews with business leaders.

Amy resides in Portland, Oregon with her husband, two children, dog and cat.

www.ingramcontent.com/pod-product-compliance
Lightning Source LLC
Chambersburg PA
CBHW071601210326
41597CB00019B/3346